ME FATHER WAS THE KEEPER:
John Smeaton and
the Eddystone Light

by

Anonymous

With Forward by
Tom Grundner

Fireship Press
www.FireshipPress.com

Me Father was the Keeper: John Smeaton and the Eddystone Light - Copyright © 2008 by Fireship Press

ISBN-13: 978-1-934757-28-4
ISBN-10: 1-934757-28-4

BISAC Subject Headings:
  BIO015000 - BIOGRAPHY & AUTOBIOGRAPHY / Science & Technology
  HIS015000 - HISTORY / Europe / Great Britain
  ARC005070 - ARCHITECTURE / History / Modern (late 19th Century
      to 1945)

This work is based on the 1876 edition of *The Story of John Smeaton and the Eddystone Lighthouse,* an Anonymous work published by Thomas Nelson and Sons, London.

1.0

ME FATHER WAS THE KEEPER:
John Smeaton and
the Eddystone Light

ABOUT CONTEMPORIZED CLASSICS™

Books from the Victorian era and earlier were written quite differently than today's works. The paragraphing, sentence structure, terminology, spelling and other factors are not what we're used to seeing. As a result, too often they jar the reader into putting the book down—or not picking it up at all. They simply do not "read right" to the modern eye.

We have taken a different approach in producing our "Contemporized Classics." Each book in this series has been edited so that long rambling sentences and paragraphs are divided into shorter ones, some sentence structures and terms are updated, and so forth. The idea is to present a work that looks and reads in a more modern, more familiar, style. These are *not* abridged works in the usual sense. If wording has been altered or cut, it is only to enhance modern readability. Indeed, great care has been taken to make sure that meaning has in no way been altered.

In many respects this process is similar to the "colorization revolution" which recently took place in the film industry. With the development of digital technology in the late 1970's, filmmakers and historians were able to re-issue a large number of classic black and white films in a modern color format. The process gave these films new life by making them more acceptable to the modern viewer.

As with the colorization of films, we're sure there will be some who will consider this effort some kind of literary sacrilege. If so, they are free to read these books in their original form. There are plenty of those volumes around.

For everyone else, welcome to the world of Contemporized Classics. If you can read these books and have the impression that they were written only yesterday, then we will have done our job.

Read them again for the first time... and enjoy!

Contents

Forward

Like most Americans, I had never heard of the Eddystone light, at least not until a song came along. And, even then, I didn't know much about it until I wrote a book.

The song was very popular in the 60's and early 70's. (Egads! I've just irretrievably dated myself.) It was called "Me Father was the Keeper of the Eddystone Light"; and it had one of those melodies that, once you hear it, will keep popping up in your brain at the oddest moments for the next week.

But I really didn't know much more about the lighthouse then its name. That was remedied in 2006 when I wrote *The Ramage Companion*, a companion book to the 18 volume series of nautical adventure novels by Dudley Pope. The lighthouse kept being mentioned in the books, so I thought I would see if there was anything interesting in its history that I could write about.

Interesting? Was it ever!

So, when I was asked to write a forward to this book, I returned to what I had written several years ago for the "Companion." What I quickly found out was that there was no way that I could edit my original words without that bloody song running through my head at the same time.

I finally gave up on trying to block it out. If I was going to be plagued by it, so should my readers—at least those who are familiar with it.

* * *

Me father was the keeper of the Eddystone light,
He married a mermaid one fine night.
And from that union there came three,
A porpoise and a porgy and the other was me.

You would not need to use its name. If you just said: 50° 10' N 04° 15'W any North Atlantic mariner would know ex-

i

actly what you meant. It's the location of The Eddystone, one of the most feared and yet romanticized rock formations in the world.

The Eddystone is a collection of 15 rocks poking out of the Atlantic Ocean. There is nothing particularly special about that, however, except for their location—and what a location it is. They sit about ten miles out to sea and guard Plymouth Harbor like a goalkeeper. If you want to enter Plymouth from almost any direction, in fair weather or foul, you must get past them; something hundreds of ships over the centuries have failed to do.

To warn mariners of its position, four lighthouses have been built—each with a story more strange than the previous one.

* * *

One night, as I was a-trimming the glim
 And singing a verse from the evening hymn
I heard a voice cry out an "Ahoy!"
 And there was me mother, sittin' on a buoy.

The first person to try to tame the Eddystone was Henry Winstanley, a wealthy, eccentric merchant and one very irate man. It seems Henry had invested a ton of money in shipping. More specifically, he had invested in a ship that had recently gone aground on the Eddystone; and he vowed to rid the seas, once and for all, of this hazard.

He started work on an octagonal wooden lighthouse in 1696 and work was progressing nicely when, in 1697, a French privateer raided the place. England and France were at war at the time so poor Henry was hauled off to Paris in chains. Eventually, King Louis XIV heard about his capture and immediately sent an emissary to the prison to secure his release. Apologizing to Mr. Winstanley, the King said: "We are at war with England, not with humanity." Such was the importance of building the Eddystone light.

The first operational lighthouse was completed in 1699 and it was a marvel of 17th century engineering. Winstanley used to brag that there was no storm that could possibly knock it down. To prove his point, in November 1703, he went out to the lighthouse to experience being in it during a tempest. Unfortunately, he picked what would later be called the "storm of the century" for his experiment. The following morning there was no light, no lighthouse, and no Henry Winstanley. The rock had been scoured clean.

* * *

"Oh, what has become of my children three?"
My mother she did ask of me.
One was exhibited as a talking fish
The other was served on a chafing dish.

If Henry Winstanley was an angry man, Colonel John Lovett was a shrewd one. He wanted to build a lighthouse, true; but decided first to secure a 99-year lease on the Eddystone rocks from Parliament. This entitled him, once the lighthouse was built, to charge a "passing toll" of one penny per ton to all ships going by. Unfortunately, how he planned to collect this preposterous toll is lost in the mist of time.

Nevertheless, he engaged John Rudyerd to design the lighthouse and in 1709 it was completed. Making it a cone shape, it proved to be very serviceable for the next 47 years when, much to the discomfort of one Henry Hall, it burned down.

Henry Hall was a 94-year-old watch keeper who was on duty the night of December 2, 1755 when the lighthouse caught fire. He and his colleagues did their best to put the fire out, but it had started in the lantern so Mr. Hall had the unenviable task of putting out a fire by throwing water UP in the air. Not good.

To make matters worse, the lighthouse had a lead roof that was melting at the same time Mr. Hall was fighting the fire. As he was tossing water up, molten lead was raining down. After the fire was over, he claimed he would have done better at fighting it except, at one point, he was looking up with his mouth open and some of the melted lead dropped straight down his throat. To say people were skeptical would be an understatement.

Not long after this, Henry Hall died. A Doctor Spry of Portsmouth conducted a post-mortem and found a flat oval piece of lead in Mr. Hall's stomach weighing over seven ounces. It can be seen to this day in the National Museum of Scotland.

* * *

Then the phosphorus flashed in her seaweed hair.
I looked again, and me mother wasn't there
But her voice came angrily out of the night
"May the devil take the keeper of the Eddystone
Light!"

By this point it was obvious that a lighthouse on the Eddystone was a much-needed thing; and they moved quickly to build another one. This is the lighthouse that would have been seen by Nelson, Sir Sidney Smith, Thomas Cochrane and the other great heros of the Napoleonic era.

Yorkshireman, John Smeaton, built this third lighthouse and it immediately captured the attention of all England. Smeaton's problem was twofold. First, how do you design a structure that will withstand the worst weather the North Atlantic can throw at it; and second, how do you build it so that it will carry an open flame 24 hours a day, yet will not burn down no matter what?

To solve the first problem, Smeaton looked to nature. What was the strongest living structure he knew of? Answer? The English oak tree, of course. So, he designed his lighthouse tower in the shape of an oak tree trunk. This alone was enough to win the hearts of any true Britain; but, more, it became the standard design that is used in lighthouses to this day.

The second problem was tougher. To make a building that would not burn you needed to construct it out of stone. Getting the stone was easy enough. There was plenty of it on the Cornish coast. Putting it together, however, was another matter. Where do you get cement that will dry quickly in wet conditions? How do you dovetail the stone so that each piece will fit together for maximum strength? For that matter, how do you lift those huge stones from the deck of a rocking ship to set them in place at all?

But if Smeaton was anything, he was ingenious. He devised his own formula for quick drying cement (which he patented). He devised a method of dovetailing stone (which is still used today). And, as for lifting the stone? Well, the stones got there, didn't they?

The lighthouse eventually had to be dismantled—a mere 120 years later. Notice I used the word "dismantled" and not "demolished," because it was literally hauled stone-by-stone to Plymouth, England where it was reassembled on Plymouth Hoe. It is now one of the town's main tourist attractions.

The current Eddystone light is a fully automated, electrified, affair complete with a helicopter deck. I know that's a good thing and it had to happen; but, I have a problem with the fact that the new lighthouse is completely unmanned.

There is thus no longer a "keeper of the Eddystone light," and there is something faintly sad about that.

* * * * *

I have edited and done forwards for books written by people I didn't personally know, but this is the first time I've done it for a book whose author is completely UN-known.

The original version was a part of a series of books published by Thomas Nelson and Sons in the late 1800's called the "Lessons from Noble Lives" series. Included, among others, were books on a naturalist, an arctic explorer, a prison reformer, and the subject of this book—John Smeaton.

Unfortunately, none of the authors of any of the books in this series were identified.

Tom Grundner
Tucson, AZ

CHAPTER ONE
Ancient and Modern Lighthouses

MAN must have recognized the necessity of lighthouses as soon as he began to go down to the sea in ships. If not lighthouses as we think of them, at least some system of signals which might guide his course at night when approaching a perilous coast, or seeking to enter a particular harbor.

His first attempt in this direction was probably nothing more than the kindling of a huge fire on some elevated promontory or headland, or on the summit of some lofty hill, where its warning glare could be seen for miles around. But as, on windy nights, much difficulty would be experienced in keeping up the blown and scattered flames, no doubt he would soon conceive the idea of providing the fire with a shelter.

So obvious was the value of these fiery beacons, and so impossible did it seem to the ancient mariner to navigate the dangerous seas without their help, that he was led to ascribe their origin to supernatural wisdom. According to the Greeks, they were invented by Hercules. There is good reason to believe, however, that long before the ocean was furrowed by a Greek keel, light-towers or fire-beacons had been erected by the Libyans and the Cuthites along the low and perilous shores of Lower Egypt. During the day they served as landmarks, and during the night as beacons. Their purpose being essentially sacred, they were also used as temples, and dedicated to the gods. Regarded by the seaman with reverence as well as gratitude, he enriched them with costly offerings.

Some authorities believe that charts of the Mediterranean coast and of the channels of the Nile were painted on these early lighthouse walls, and were later transferred to sheets of papyrus. We know that the priests in charge of them taught the sciences of hydrography and pilotage, and how to steer a vessel's course by the aid of the stars and planets.

On the summit a fire was continuously burning; the fuel being placed in an iron or bronze device with three or four branches. Each branch represented a dolphin or some other marine animal, and all were connected by decorative work. The machine was fastened to the extremity of a strong pole or shaft, like a mast, and placed so that its light was mainly directed seaward.

The impression which the fire-towers produced on the mind is finely described by Homer in a well-known passage of the *Iliad*:

> As to seamen o'er the wave is borne
> The watch-fire's light, which, high among the hills,
> Some shepherd kindles in his lonely fold.

It is said that the first regular light-tower, was erected by one Lesches, on the Sigaean promontory, at the mouth of the Hellespont. While it was the most ancient, its design was not passed down to its successors. This honor was bestowed on the celebrated tower erected on the island of Pharos, off the harbor of Alexandria, which served as a model for some of the noblest lighthouses built in later ages. It was, for example, the model used by the Emperor Claudius in the pharos raised at Ostia, near the mouth of the Tiber, which appears to have been the most complete of any on the Italian coast.

This pharos was situated on a breakwater, or artificial island, which occupied the mid-channel between the two massive piers that formed the harbor, and its ruins were visable as late as the fifteenth century, when they were visited by Pope Pius II.

Scarcely inferior in architectural excellence was the pharos which led the homeward-bound into the prosperous harbor of Puteoli; or that which Augustus erected at Ravenna; or that which from the mole of Messina poured its useful splendor over the seething waters of Charybdis; or that which embellished the island of Caprese, the favorite retreat of Tiberius, and which was destroyed by an earthquake shortly before the emperor's death.

We read of a famous lighthouse at the mouth of the river Chrysorrhoas, which flows into the Thracian Bosporus (i.e., the Strait of Constantinople). On the crest of the hill washed by this river may be seen the Timean Tower, a tower of extraordinary height, whose summit commands a wide expanse of sea. It was been built for the safety of the navigator, and fires were kindled upon it for his guidance; a precaution made all the more necessary because the shores of this strait are without ports, and no anchor can reach the bottom. But it wasn't long before the barbarians in the neighborhood figured out that if they lit other fires upon elevated points of the coast, mariners would be deceived and wreck their ships, which the barbarians could then loot.

The pharos, or lighthouse, at Alexandria, to which we have referred, was built by an architect named Sostrates, in the reign, it is said, of Ptolemseus Philadelphus. The island on which it stood lay in front of the wealthy city of Alexandria, so as to protect both its harbors, the Greater Harbor and the Haven of Happy Return, from the northern gales, and the inrush of the Mediterranean.

It forms a ledge of dazzlingly white calcareous rock, the northern slope of which is fringed with islets, which, in the fourth and fifth centuries of our era, were inhabited by Christian hermits. A deep inlet on that side was called the Pirates' Creek, because, in very early times, it had been the home of the Carian and Samian sea-rovers.

The island was connected with the mainland by an artificial mound, or causeway, which, from its extent, seven stadia (about three-quarters of a mile), was called the Heptastadium. Along its length a couple of breaks occurred, to allow of the passage of the waters, and each break was spanned by a drawbridge. At one end of the island stood a temple dedicated to Hephsestos, the god of fire, and, at the other, the great Gate of the Moon. The lighthouse was erected at the eastern end, on a kind of rocky peninsula; and as it was built of white stone and of considerable height, it was both a notable landmark from the low sandy Egyptian plains as well as from the surrounding waters.

It is generally believed that this splendid tower, which is estimated to have measured from 550 to 580 feet in height, fell into decay between 1200 and 1300, and was finally destroyed by the Turkish conquerors of Egypt. That it existed in the twelfth century, we know from the description given by an Arab writer, named Edrisi:

"This pharos," he says, "has not its equal in the world, for skill of construction or for solidity; since, to say nothing of the fact that it is built of the best stone, its separate layers of masonry are cemented together by molten lead, and this so firmly, that the whole is indissoluble, though the northern waves incessantly beat against it. From the rock to the middle gallery or stage the measurement is exactly seventy fathoms; and from this gallery to the summit, twenty-six fathoms.

"We ascend to the gallery by an inner staircase of sufficient width. This staircase goes no further, and the building, from the gallery upwards, decreases considerably in diameter. In the interior, and under the staircase, some chambers have been built. From the gallery we continue our ascent by a very narrow flight of steps: in every part it is pierced with loopholes, to give light to persons making use of it, and to assist them in obtaining a proper footing.

"This edifice is singularly remarkable, as much on account of its height as of its massiveness. It is of exceeding usefulness, its fire burning night and day for the guidance of navigators. They are well acquainted with its light, and steer their course accordingly, for it is visible at the distance of a day's sail.[1] During the night it shines like a star; by day you can distinguish it by its smoke."

Lighthouses or beacons were first introduced into England by the Romans, to whom we are indebted for so much that is valuable and useful. On the crest of the high hill at Dover still stands the pharos, which is supposed to have been built for the guidance of vessels from the coasts of France to the Roman station at Portus Rutupise (now Richborough) near Sandwich, or to Regulbium (now known as the Reculvers) on the Thames.

At the present day it is nothing more than a massive shell. In the inside the walls are vertical and squared; on the outside, they incline to assume a conical form. Of the building, as we now see it, only the basement is of Roman work; the octagonal chamber above was constructed in the reign of Henry VIII. The dimensions are about fourteen feet square.

The English beacons were of a more primitive construction than the Roman. We read in Lambarde, the old topographer, that "before the time of King Edward III. they were made of great stacks of wood; but about the eleventh year of his reign it was ordained that in one shire [Kent] they should be high standards, with their pitch-pots—that is, tall masts—to whose summit was fastened a vessel full of burning pitch. Those beacons, however, were more frequently used to warn the country of the approach of a hostile fleet than for the purpose of lighting the coasts, though, doubtlessly, they answered both objects."

---

[1] There is, of course, some exaggeration here.

Professor Faraday suggests that the first idea of a lighthouse was the candle in the cottage window, guiding the husband across the water or the pathless moor. The main point to be secured was a steady light, and it mattered not whether this was obtained from pitch-pots, coals, or oil. Wood, however, as the material most available, was most generally used.

The Tour de Cordouan, situated at the mouth of the Gironde, was long lit by wood fires; while, until a comparatively recent period, the lighthouses at Spurn Head, north of the Humber, and on the Isle of May, at the entrance to the Firth of Forth, were lighted by braziers of burning coal.

Our English Kings were quick to perceive the importance of insuring greater safety to the vessels composing their commercial navy. In 1525, Henry VIII. granted a charter to the "brotherhood of the Holy Trinity" (now known as Trinity House), for the purpose of assisting and protecting navigation by licensing and regulating pilots, and planting beacons, lighthouses, and buoys along the British coasts. But, as Mr. Smiles remarks, the only step taken to carry out these plans was the granting of leases by the Crown. These were granted for a fixed number of years, to private persons willing to find the means of building and maintaining lights. In return they had permission to levy tolls on all passing shipping. Yet, even with that incentive, not much was done to render our dangerous coasts easier and safer to approach.

The first light tower was on Dungeness in the reign of James I. About the same time some parts of the Cornish coast were lighted up. We read in the *Travels of the Grand Duke Cosmo*, about two centuries ago, that the Plymouth shipping paid four pence per ton for the lights which were in the lighthouses at night. Four pence in those days was worth about as much as five shillings in our own, so that the tax must have fallen mostly on merchantmen. [Ed. This would be about $6 per ton in 2007 U.S. dollars]

It is also recorded, in the annals of the old town of Rye,

that a light was hung out from the southeast angle of the Ypres Tower, as a guide for vessels entering the harbor in the night time. This proving insufficient, another light was ordered by the corporation "to be hung out o' nights on the southwest corner of the church, for a guide to vessels entering the port." A pitch-pot was formerly hung from the spire of old Arundel Church, as a beacon for vessels which wished to enter the port of Little Hampton, and the iron support of the apparatus can still be seen.

It is obvious that lights such as these were something less than ideal. It was difficult to maintain an equable radiance; they were not visible far out at sea; and they were easily affected by variations of weather—great gales, tempests, or thick mists. Moreover, as navigation increased, and ships more frequently threaded the narrow pass or dangerous channel, more lights became necessary. Thus the old system of lights had to give way to a more regular and extensive lighthouse system.

The first lighthouse of a solid and permanent character was built, it is said, at Lowestoft in Suffolk, in 1609. In 1665 one was erected at Hunstanton Point; and in 1680, a third on the Scilly Isles. About the same time were established the lighthouses at Dungeness and Orfordness. But all these were of clumsy construction, of very slight elevation, and of weak illuminating power.

To inaugurate the modern lighthouse the genius of John Smeaton was needed. From the date of his marvelous monument on the Eddystone Rock up to the present time, nearly every dangerous point of our coasts, every harbor and every river-mouth, has been included in a national lighthouse system.

CHAPTER TWO
A Mechanic from Leeds

JOHN SMEATON was born at Austhorpe Lodge, near Leeds, on the 8th of June 1724. His father was a respectable attorney, who came of an old Yorkshire family; his mother was a quick-witted, firm, gentle-mannered woman. He was taught at home during his earlier years, and a happy home it was.

Leeds, in those days, had not attained to its present immense proportions, and Austhorpe was completely in the country, sheltered by the noble park and overhanging woods of Temple-Newsham. There was ample room for the healthy, active boy, to indulge himself in his favorite pursuits, which all had a mechanical character. He was never so happy, says one of his biographers, as when put in possession of any cutting tool, by which he could make his little imitations of houses, pumps, and wind-mills.

Even while still in petticoats, he was continually dividing circles and squares; and the only playthings in which he took a genuine pleasure were his working models. If any carpenters or masons chanced to be employed in the neighborhood of Austhorpe, the boy was sure to find his way amongst them; and there he would spend hour after hour, watching the men at work, and observing how they handled their tools. Holmes tells us that, having one day taken due note of the operations of some mill-wrights, shortly afterwards, to the terror of his family, he was seen fixing a rude likeness of a wind-mill on the top of his father's barn.

Another time, when watching the procedure of a party of men engaged in fixing the village pump, he was fortunate enough to obtain from them a piece of bored pipe, which he succeeded in fastening into a working-pump that actually raised water.

At a proper age, the boy was sent to the Leeds grammar-school, where he received, it is supposed, the largest part of his school instruction. In geometry and arithmetic he made very rapid progress but, as is the case with most clever and industrious boys, he learned more at home than at school. Every leisure moment was occupied by his tools and machines.

He acquired, in time, a mechanical dexterity and ingenuity which were really surprising, and availed him in the performance of some amusing surprises. Thus, it happened that some mechanics came into the neighborhood to erect a "fire-engine," as the steam-engine was then called, for the purpose of pumping water from the Garforth coal-mines, and day after day Smeaton visited the spot for the purpose of watching their operations.

Carefully examining their methods, he made use of the knowledge so acquired to construct a miniature engine at home, appropriately equipped with pumps and other apparatus; and he even succeeded in setting it in motion before the colliery engine was completed. He first tried its powers upon one of the fish-ponds in front of the house at Austhorpe, which he quickly contrived to pump dry, and so killed all the fish in it, greatly to the surprise as well as the annoyance of his father.

Working on in this way, with assiduous application, young Smeaton, by the time he had arrived at his fifteenth year, had made a turning-lathe, on which he turned wood and ivory; and it was his delight to make presents of little boxes and other articles of his own manufacture to his friends. He also learned to work in metals, which he fused and forged without any assistance; and by the age of eighteen he handled his tools as dexterously as any regular smith or joiner.

"In the year 1742," says Mr. Holmes, his biographer and friend, "I spent a month at his father's house; and being intended myself for a mechanical employment, and a few years younger than he was, I could not but view his works with astonishment. He forged his iron and steel, and melted his metaL He had tools of every sort for working in wood, ivory, and metals. He had made a lathe, by which he cut a perpetual screw in brass—a thing little known at that day, and which, I believe, was the invention of Mr. Henry Hindley of York, with whom I served my apprenticeship. Mr. Smeaton soon became acquainted with him, and spent many a night at Mr. Hindley's house until daylight, conversing on these subjects."

In his sixteenth year, our hero—for every biographer must have a hero—was removed from school to his father's office, where he was engaged in the uncongenial task of copying dreary legal folios, and acquiring as much knowledge of law as might fit him for an attorney's profession. As Mr. Smeaton had a good connection in Leeds, he not unnaturally wished his son to profit by it; but the future engineer revolted from "Blackstone's Commentaries" and "Coke upon Littleton." Like a good son, he attended assiduously to his office duties, every day he found the burden of a detested occupation heavier to bear.

Towards the end of 1742, partly with the view of furthering his professional duties, and partly for the sake of taking him away from his all-engrossing mechanical pursuits, Mr. Smeaton sent him to London. Here he made an attempt to conform his tastes to his father's wishes; but utterly failing, he wrote to him an earnest appeal for permission to follow what was clearly an unconquerable bias.

With equal kindness and wisdom, his father consented, and young Smeaton immediately entered the service of a philosophical instrument-maker. He applied himself to his new vocation with such admirable energy, and it was so entirely fitted to the measure of his talents, that in a very short time he was able to relieve his father from all expenses connected with his maintenance.

It is not to be supposed that a young man with so much strength of purpose and clearness of intellect would devote himself only to the mechanical part of his profession. He read industriously and methodically, so as to obtain a knowledge of the principles of theoretical science; he sought the society of educated men; he regularly attended the meetings and lectures of the Royal Society. He started in business on his own account in 1750, when he was only twenty-six; and in the same year he read a paper before the Royal Society on certain improvements effected by himself and Dr. Knight in the mariner's compass. In 1751 he invented a machine to measure a ship's way at sea, and experimented with it in a voyage down the Thames, and in a short cruise on board the *Fortune* sloop-of-war.

The activity and fertility of his mind are abundantly demonstrated by the nature of the work which occupied him in the following year.

In April we read of a paper from his pen detailing certain improvements which he had contrived in the air-pump; in June he describes an ingenious modification in ship-tackle by means of pulleys, so arranged that one man might easily raise a ton weight.

In November he describes certain experiments which had been made with Captain Savary's steam-engine, the precursor of James Watt's. Meantime he was engaged in researches into "the Natural Powers of Water and Wind to Turn Mills and other Machines depending on a Circular Motion;" which afterwards gained him the Royal Society's gold medal—almost the highest honor a man of science can receive in England.

Now, it is obvious that to accomplish so much honest and valuable work, and at the same time to carry on his business, required great application, great energy, great method. And it must be conceded that throughout life Smeaton was an unwearied seeker after knowledge; and that his two main objects were, self-improvement and the public welfare. Self-improvement was necessary that he might render the gifts he possessed of the highest possible usefulness to society.

"One of his maxims," says Smiles, "was, that 'the abilities of the individual are a debt owed to the common stock of public happiness.' The steadfastness with which he devoted himself to useful work, in which he at the same time found his own true happiness, shows that the maxim was no mere lip-service on his part, but formed the very mainspring of his life. From an early period he carefully laid out his time with a view to getting the most good out of it: so much for study, so much for practical experiments, so much for business, and so much for rest and relaxation."

Let the young reader take note of this, and in like manner find for everything its fitting and sufficient time. There is much wisdom in the adage, "A place for everything, and everything in its place;" but it is equally necessary that there should be "an hour for everything, and everything in its hour."

The best talents, the best opportunities, will be wholly wasted, unless their possessor can recognize the value of method. The man who does not systematize his time, who does not economize it so as to accomplish in each day the largest possible amount of work, without haste or unhealthy pressure, will make but an indifferent use of his gifts, and will assuredly lose many precious hours.

He will always be too late; always endeavoring to overtake the lost moments, and never succeeding in doing so. At length such a weight will accumulate upon him of work undone and opportunities missed, that, in his exhaustion and discontent, he will lose all hope, and sink into the idleness of apathy.

Method is the secret of success: the methodical student will get out of the twenty-four hours all that it is possible to get out of them; while the irregular and disorderly will lose a more or less considerable portion of them, according to the degree of his want of system.

Smeaton devoted a portion of his time to the study of French, in order that he might be able to read the valuable scientific treatises contained in that language, and also that he might be able to take a journey which he contemplated into the Low Countries, for the purpose of inspecting the great canal works of the Dutch engineers.

He carried out his intention in 1754, when he traversed Holland and Belgium—mostly on foot, or in the *truckschuyts* or canal boats, which form the national conveyance of those countries—and carefully inspected the most remarkable achievements of mechanical science in the districts through which he passed.

It was with no little interest he found himself in a land which has been literally rescued from the sea by the efforts of human skill and industry; a great portion of which, even in comparatively modern times, was buried deep beneath the waters of ocean; a land to which nature has been so unkindly, and for which man has done so much. In a certain sense, Holland is the creation, as well as the trophy, of the engineer; and wherever Smeaton went, he found himself in the engineer's track. From Rotterdam he travelled by Delft, famous for its pottery, and the Hague, to the great commercial emporium of Amsterdam, and thence, as far north as Helder, examining with critical attention the huge dikes and embankments raised by the labor of man to prevent the sea from recovering its own.

At Amsterdam he saw with delight and surprise its admirable harbor and spacious docks. In Smeaton's time, London had nothing like it. The numerous fleets which flocked to the British metropolis simply dropped anchor in the Thames, and loaded and unloaded at the river quays.

Passing round the country by Utrecht, he proceeded to inspect the great sea-sluices at Brill and Helvoetsluys, through which the inland waters found a channel of egress, while the billows of ocean were prevented from forcing an entrance. During this journey he made copious notes of all he saw, and the information thus acquired was of great use to him in his after-labors as a canal and harbor engineer.

He returned to England in 1755; and shortly afterwards the opportunity came to him which, we believe, comes to every man of industrious habits and steadfast purpose—the opportunity, by a prudent employment of which, we may place ourselves in a position to turn our gifts to good account, and do something for the advantage of our fellows.

The lighthouse erected by Rudyerd on the Eddystone Rock was swept away by a destructive fire on the 2nd of December, and it became necessary to replace it with a new one. The proprietors applied to the President of the Royal Society to recommend to them an engineer who might be safely entrusted with a work so important.

The then President, the Earl of Macclesfield, replied "that there was one of their own body whom he could venture to recommend for the work; yet that the most material part of what he knew of him was his having, within the compass of the last seven years, recommended himself to the Society by the communication of several mechanical contrivances and improvements; and though he had at first made it his business to execute things in the instrument way (without ever having been bred to the trade), yet, on account of the merit of his performances, he had been chosen a member of the Society; and that, for about three years past, having found the business of a scientific instrument maker not likely to afford an adequate recompense, he had wholly applied himself to various branches of mechanics."

Upon this recommendation the proprietors acted, and Smeaton was engaged to erect the Eddystone lighthouse.

CHAPTER THREE
First Attempts at the Eddystone

ABOUT fourteen miles to the southwest of Plymouth harbor, and out in the deep and billowy channel, lies a reef or ledge of rocks, known, in allusion to the swirl of currents always tossing and seething around it, by the name of the Eddystone.

This reef is situated in a line with Lizard Head in Cornwall, and Start Point in Devonshire. Consequently, it forms a perilous obstruction, not only in the water-way which leads to the great arsenal and haven of South Devon, but in the track of all vessels entering or leaving the English Channel; which, we may add, is frequented by a greater number of ships than any other part of the wide ocean.

When the tide is up, its hoary crest is scarcely visible, but its position is shown by the eddy which washes to and fro above it; at low tide, several low, jagged, and dreary ridges of gneiss rock lift their heads from the boiling waves. During a stiff breeze from the southwest, these form the centre, the focus, as it were, of a boiling caldron of waters, and no ship enticed within their vortex can escape destruction.

As may be supposed, the erection of a lighthouse on rocks

so perilous came to be regarded as an urgent need soon after men had learned the value of commercial enterprise. The task, however, seemed so dangerous, not to say impossible, that no one ventured to attempt it, until 1696, when it was undertaken by a noble and patriotic gentleman, named Henry Winstanley, who was much grieved by the loss of life which annually occurred there.

Winstanley is described as one of those eccentric but ingenious men who find a peculiar pleasure in mystifying their friends, and in throwing a kind of glamour or magical atmosphere over our daily, commonplace, realistic life. He made use of his scientific knowledge to play the most extraordinary practical jokes.

You go to spend a night or two at his old Essex manor-house. On entering your bed-room, you nearly tripped over an old slipper. You kicked it aside, and, lo, a ghost immediately started from the floor. In your sudden alarm you flung yourself into the nearest chair: out sprang a couple of arms, and clasped you and held you a prisoner. You went into the garden, and sought repose in a woodbine-trellised arbour. Your seat and yourself shot away from the pleasant alcove, and were quickly floating in the middle of the adjoining canal!

The author of such devices as these might be, and was, a noble and chivalrous gentleman, but he was also, unquestionably, a very eccentric character! His eccentricity displayed itself in the lighthouse which his chivalrous humanity instigated him to build on the Eddystone Rock. On first glancing at an engraving of it, you hardly know whether you see before you a Chinese pagoda or a Turkish minaret, grafted on a circular tower, and ornamented with cranes and chains like a London warehouse!

Winstanley began his work in 1696.

The first summer—and, of course, it was only in summer that men could labor on that windswept, wave-worn rock—

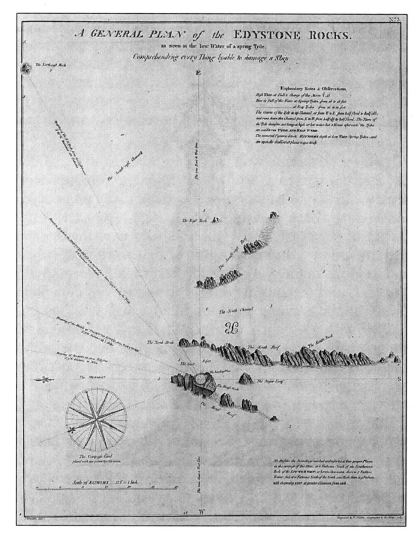

*An 18th Century Map of the
Eddystone Rocks*

was occupied in excavating twelve holes, and fastening as many irons in them, to serve for the superstructure.

Very slowly and drearily did the work go on; for though it was the "sweet summer-time," out in the wild channel the weather would frequently prove of such terrible violence that, for ten or fourteen days in succession, the waters would boil and toss about the rocks. Vexed by contrary winds, and by the inrush of the swelling billows from the main ocean. the waves mount one upon another, like maddened horses, and leap and bound to such a height as completely to bury the reef and all upon it, effectively preventing any vessel or boat from drawing near. On such days the men, you may be sure, thanked God that they were housed safely on the green shores of Devon.

The second summer was spent in building up a solid circular mass of masonry, twelve feet high and fourteen feet in diameter. In the third summer this huge pillar was enlarged two feet at the base, and the superstructure was carried up to a height of sixty feet. "Being all finished," says the engineer, "with the lantern, and all the rooms that were in it, we ventured to lodge in the work. But the first night the weather became bad, and so continued, that it was eleven days before any boats could come near us again; and not being acquainted with the height of the sea's rising, we were almost drowned with wet, and our provisions in as bad a condition, though we worked day and night as much as possible to make shelter for ourselves. In this storm we lost some of our materials, although we did what we could to save them; but the boat then returning, we all left the house, to be refreshed on shore: and as soon as the weather did permit we returned and finished all, and put up the light on the 14th November 1698; which being so late in the year, it was three days before Christmas before we had relief to go on shore again, and were almost at the last extremity for want of provisions; but, by good Providence, then two boats came with provisions and the family that was to take care of the light; and so ended this year's work."

In the course of the fourth summer the foundations were considerably strengthened, and the remainder of the work pertaining to the fabric itself was completed. We are told, and the extant engravings show us, that it bore, in its finished condition, a close resemblance to "a Chinese pagoda, with open galleries and fantastic projections."

Around the lantern ran a wide open gallery; so wide and open, indeed, that it was possible, when the sea ran high, for a six-oared boat to be lifted up by the waves and driven through it. Such an edifice could not long withstand the violence of the gale or the fury of the waters; but this much was

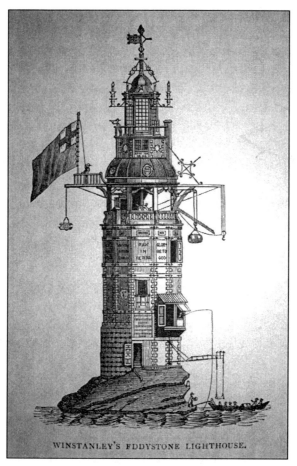

WINSTANLEY'S EDDYSTONE LIGHTHOUSE.

Winstanley's Lighthouse
1699

gained by its construction. It was shown that a lighthouse could be erected on this sea-girt rock, and, therefore, the achievement deserves to be described as "one of the most laudable enterprises which any heroic mind could undertake, for it filled the breast of the mariner with new hope."

Winstanley was very proud of his work, and so convinced, it is said, of its thorough stability, that he frequently expressed a wish to be under its roof in the fiercest hurricane that ever blew beneath the face of heaven, assured that it would not shake one joist or beam. Heaven sometimes takes the presumptuous at their word!

Winstanley, with his workmen and light-keepers, had fixed his residence in the tower, when a tremendous storm arose, which, on the 24th of November, 1703, blew a hurricane of unprecedented violence. The sea rolled its billows heavily, and the wind raged, and masses of cloud darkened the horizon, and all Nature seemed convulsed by the elemental strife.

When the dawn broke on the 27th, the people of Plymouth hastened to the beach, and turned their anxious gaze towards the Eddystone. The waters swirled and seethed around and about the rock; but where was the lighthouse, the fantastic structure raised by the ready brain and daring soul of Winstanley?

During the night it had been swept away, and not a memorial remained of its ill-fated occupants.

The melancholy incident forms the theme of a striking ballad by Jean Ingelow, which concludes in the following manner:

> And it fell out, fell out at last,
>   That he would put to sea,
> To scan once more his lighthouse-tower
>   On the rock o' destiny.
>
> And the winds woke, and the storm broke,
>   And wrecks came plunging in;
> None in the town that night lay down
>   Or sleep or rest to win.
>
> The great mad waves were rolling graves,
>   And each flung up its dead;
> The seething flow was white below,
>   And black the sky overhead.

And when the dawn, the dull gray dawn.
    Broke on the trembling town,
And men looked south to the harbor mouth,
    The lighthouse-tower was down!

Down in the deep where he doth sleep
    Who made it shine afar,
And then in the night that drowned its light,
    Set, with his pilot star.

The usefulness of a beacon on the Eddystone Rock had been so abundantly proved that it was not long before an attempt was made to replace Winstanley's unfortunate structure.

A Captain Lovett obtained a ninety-nine years' lease of the rock from the Trinity House Corporation, and engaged as his architect a silk-mercer on Ludgate Hill, named John Rudyerd. The reasons that led him to make so curious a choice are unknown, but the event proved that it was a sensible one. Rudyerd designed a graceful and even elegant building, choosing a circle for the outline, and studying the greatest simplicity, so as to offer the least possible resistance to wind and wave.

In order to obtain a firm foundation, he divided the surface of the rock into seven slightly unequal stages, and in these he dug or excavated thirty-six holes, varying in depth from twenty to thirty inches. Each hole was six inches square at the top, gradually narrowing to five inches, and then again expanding and flattening to nine inches by three at the bottom. Into these dove-tailed cavities or sockets were inserted strong iron bolts, weighing from two to five hundredweight, according to length and structure.

These bolts held fast a course of squared oak timbers laid lengthwise on the lowest of the seven stages, so as to reach the level of the stage or step immediately above it. Another set of beams was then laid diagonally covering those already laid, and raising the level surface to the height of the third stage. The next course was deposited longitudinally, and the fourth diagonally, and so on alternately, until a basement of solid timber was erected, two courses higher than the highest point of the rock.

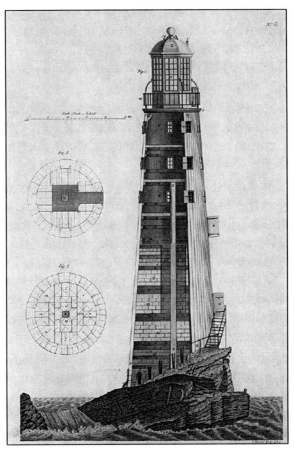

Rudyerd's Lighthouse
1709

Rudyerd's lighthouse is generally described as a fabric of wood; but this is incorrect. To obtain the necessary solidity, and a sufficient weight to counteract the weight of the waters of the Channel, he combined courses of Cornish granite with his courses of timber, in the proportion of five to two. So, for example, he laid two courses of timber, and then five of granite, and then two more of timber; all being firmly secured by iron bolts and cramps. On this substructure, which measured

63 feet in height, with a base of 23 feet, he raised four stories of timber, crowned by an octagonal lantern, 10 feet 6 inches in diameter, and a ball of 2 feet 3 inches in diameter. The total elevation, from the lowest surface of the rock to the top of this ball, was 92 feet. Rudyerd completed his work in 1709.

For a long period of years, nearly half a century, it withstood the attacks of wind and wave, and many a vessel was kept from destruction by its warning light. On the 2nd of December 1755, it was fated to fall before an unexpected enemy.

There were three keepers resident in the lighthouse at the time. One of them, whose turn it was to watch, entered the lantern, at about two o'clock A.M., to snuff the candles, and, to his horror, discovered it to be filled with smoke. On opening the door which led to the balcony, to permit of its escape, a flame instantly leaped from the interior of the cupola. He hastened to alarm his companions, and vigorous efforts were made to extinguish the fire; but these proved ineffectual, owing to the dryness of the woodwork, and the difficulty of raising a sufficient supply of water to the top of the building. Fortunately for the keepers, the flames were seen from the shore, and a well-manned boat put off to their relief.

It reached the Eddystone about ten o'clock, when the fire had been raging for eight hours. The building was wholly destroyed. The keepers, who had been driven away by the falling beams, the red-hot iron, and molten lead, were found, in a panic-stricken condition, crouching in a recess or cavern on the east side of the rock. They were carried into the boat, and conveyed ashore.

Curious to relate, they were no sooner landed than one of them stole away, and was never afterwards heard of. His flight gave rise to a suspicion that the fire was not accidental; yet, when we remember that a lighthouse rock affords no means of escape for its inmates, we can hardly suppose it to be the place an incendiary would select for the scene of his wicked attempt. It is possible that the man's nerves had been so tried by the terrible nature of the peril he had undergone, that he knew not what he did.

Of the other two light-keepers, one, named Henry Hall, met with a singular fate. While engaged in dashing some buckets of water on the burning roof of the cupola, he chanced to look upwards, and a mass of molten lead fell down upon his head, face, and shoulders, burning him severely. On his arrival ashore, he persisted in asserting that a portion of the liquefied metal had gone down his throat.

His medical attendant regarded the assertion as the offspring of a disordered imagination; but the man rapidly grew worse, and on the twelfth day of his illness, after an attack of violent convulsions, expired. A post-mortem examination of his body then took place, and Hall's story was found to be true; for in the stomach lay a flat, oval piece of lead, seven ounces and five drachms in weight!

CHAPTER FOUR
Building the Impossible

Acting on the old maxim of "Try, try, and try again," the Trinity House Corporation determined to erect another light-tower on the Eddystone, and entrusted the work to a mathematical instrument maker, named John Smeaton, a 32 year old mechanic, who had already acquired a reputation for ingenuity.

The subject was wholly new to him, and therefore, as was his custom, he began to investigate it in detail before he took any decisive step.

On examining into the conditions of the task, he came to the conclusion that the structures of his predecessors had both been deficient in weight; and that if Rudyerd's had not been destroyed by fire, it would not have resisted the fury of the tempest much longer. He announced his intention, therefore, of raising a fabric of such solidity that the sea should give way to it, and not it to the sea; and he determined to build it entirely of stone.

Moreover, Winstanley and Rudyerd had wasted much valuable time, from the difficulty of landing on the rock, and the impossibility of working on it continuously for any length of time. But Smeaton proposed to moor a vessel within a quarter of a mile of the scene of action, which should accommodate his company of workmen; and thus they would be prepared to seize every opportunity of launching their boat, and carrying their materials to the rock, instead of making a long voyage from Plymouth on each occasion.

So far as the design of his intended erection, he was ready to adopt Rudyerd's idea of a cone, but he proposed to enlarge its diameter considerably. The picture he kept constantly before his eye was the trunk of an oak tree, which is equally remarkable for gracefulness and strength, and withstands successfully the most furious gales, when other forest trees are bent or broken.

As soon as he had made up his mind as to the principles on which the lighthouse should be constructed, he paid a visit to its intended site. He arrived at Plymouth about the end of March, but it was the 2nd of April before he could embark for the Eddystone, owing to the violence of the wind and the heavy sea that was running in the Channel.

On reaching the rock, the billows beat upon it with so much fury that it was impossible to land. All that Smeaton could do was to view the rocky cone—the mere crest of the mountain whose base was laid so far down in the sea-deeps beneath—over which the waves were lashing, and to form a more adequate idea of the very narrow as well as turbulent site on which he was expected to erect his building.

Three days later, however, he ventured on a second trip, when he succeeded in landing on the rock, and thoroughly examining it. The only traces he could find of the lighthouses erected by his predecessors were the iron branches fixed by Rudyerd, and remains of those fixed by Winstanley.

On a third voyage to the rock, Smeaton was baffled by the wind, which compelled him to return to harbor without even obtaining a sight of it. During the next five days he was employed in looking for a proper site for a work-yard, and examining the granite in the neighborhood to be used for building. He made a fourth voyage, and although the vessel reached the rock, the wind blew so freshly and the breakers dashed so furiously that it was again found impossible to land. He could only direct the boat to lie off and on, while he watched the breaking of the sea and its action on the reef.

A fifth trial, a week later, proved equally unsuccessful. After rowing about all day with the wind ahead, the party found themselves at night about four miles from the Eddystone, near which they anchored until morning; but a storm of wind and rain arising, they were compelled to return to Plymouth without succeeding reaching the rock.

The sixth attempt—we record these minute particulars because they give such a vivid illustration of Smeaton's persevering energy—was successful, and on the 22nd of April, after the lapse of seventeen days, Mr. Smeaton landed a second time.

After a careful inspection, the party retired to their sloop, which lay off until the tide had fallen, when Smeaton again landed, and the night being very calm, he continued on the rock until nine in the evening.

On the 23rd he again landed, and pursued his operations; but this time he was interrupted by the ground-swell, which dashed the waves upon the reef, and, the wind rising, the sloop was forced to put back to Plymouth. During this visit, however, our engineer had secured some fifteen hours occupation on the rock, and taken the dimensions of all its parts, to enable him to construct an accurate model of the foundation of the proposed structure. To correct the drawing, however, and to insure the utmost exactness, he determined upon attempting an eighth and final voyage of inspection on the 28th of April.

Again the violence of the sea foiled him in his design.

Another fortnight passed, a fortnight of unfavorable weather; but the time was not wasted. The engineer elaborated his design, and made all the preliminary arrangements to proceed with the work He also drew up a careful code of regulations for the instruction and government of the artificers and others who were to be employed upon it. And this being done, he arranged for a journey to London, but not until he had paid three more visits to the rock for the purpose of correcting his measurements.

The autumn of 1756 was occupied in the transport of the granite and other materials to the rock, in their preparation, and in the excavation of the steps or stages on which the foundation was to be laid.

The return of the workmen to port, in their store-vessel the *Neptune*, was safely accomplished, though the voyage was not unattended with danger.

Unable, in consequence of the violence of the gale, to make Plymouth harbor, the *Neptune* was steered for Fowey, on the coast of Cornwall. Higher and higher rose the wind, until it blew quite a storm; and in the night Mr. Smeaton, hearing a sudden alarm and outcry amongst the crew overhead, ran upon deck half-dressed to learn the cause. It was raining heavily, and the hurricane lashed the waters into a whirlpool of spray and foam.

"It being very dark," says Smeaton, "the first thing I saw was the horrible appearance of breakers almost surrounding us; John Bowden, one of the seamen, kept crying out, 'For God's sake, heave hard at that rope, if you mean to save your lives!' I immediately laid hold of the rope, at which he himself was hauling as well as the other seamen, though he was also managing the helm. I not only hauled with all my strength, but called to and encouraged the workmen to do the same thing." The sea was dashing with terrible fury, and with a roar which drowned all other sounds, upon the rock.

The *Neptune's* jib-sail was suddenly torn into a thousand shreds; and to save the main-sail, it was lowered, when, happily, the vessel obeyed her helm, swung round, and put out to sea. At daybreak her crew found themselves out of sight of land, and driving towards the Bay of Biscay. But as the gale had abated, they soon got the vessel's head round again, and stood for the coast Before night they sighted the Land's End, but could not then make the shore.

For another night and day they were tossed to and fro, almost helplessly. A vessel coming in sight, they exhibited signals of distress; she bore down, and directed them how to steer for the Scilly Islands. The wind veering round, however, they bore up again for the Land's End, passed the Lizard and Rame Head, and, finally, after being blown about at sea for four days, dropped anchor in Plymouth Sound, much to their own contentment and to the satisfaction of their friends, who were despairing of their reappearance.

* * *

Early in June 1757 the work of tower erection began. The first stone, weighing two tons five hundredweight, was laid

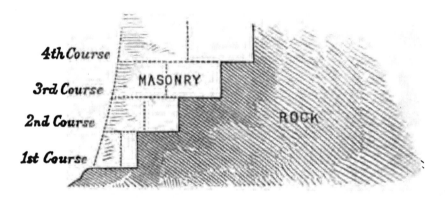

on the 12th. On the next day was finished the first course, consisting of four stones, so ingeniously dove-tailed into one another and into the rock as to form a single compact mass. The sloping form of the rock, to which the foundation was, of course, adapted, required only this small number of stones for the first course; the diameter of the masonry gradually increasing until the highest level surface was reached. Thus:

The second course, completed on the 30th of June, consisted of thirteen blocks of granite; the third course, completed on the 11th of July, of twenty-five; the fourth, on the 31st, of thirty-three. The sixth course was laid down by the

11th of August; and as it rose above the high-water mark, Smeaton was entitled to consider that he had conquered the greatest difficulties of his task.

Up to this point the mode of procedure in laying and fixing each great block of granite was as follows:

The stone to be set being hung in the tackle, and its bed of mortar spread. It was then lowered into its place, beaten with a heavy wooden mall, and leveled with a spirit-level; and the stone being accurately brought to its marks, was considered as set in its proper position.

The next thing was to keep it there, even though the utmost violence of the sea might beat upon it before the mortar was thoroughly hard and dry. Therefore the carpenter dropped into a couple of vertical grooves, which had been previously cut in "the waist" of the stone, each an inch deep and three inches wide, two oaken wedges, one upon its head, the other with its point downwards, so that the two in each groove would lie heads and points. With an iron bar, about two inches and a half broad, a quarter of an inch thick, and two feet and a half long, he then drove down one wedge upon the other—very gently at first, so that the opposite pairs of wedges, being equally tightened, would equally resist each other, and the stone would therefore keep its place.

In like manner, a couple of wedges were pitched at the top of each groove; the dormant wedge (i.e., the one with the point upward) being held in the hand, while the drift wedge (i.e., the one with the point downward) was driven with a hammer. So much as remained above the upper surface of the stone was cut away with saw or chisel; and, generally, a couple of thin wedges were driven very moderately at the butt-end of the stone, whose tendency being to force it out of its dove-tail, they would, by moderate driving, assist in preserving the steadiness of the entire mass, in opposition to any violent agitation arising from the sea.

The stone thus firmly secured, a certain portion of mortar was liquefied, and the joints having been carefully "pointed," this liquid cement was poured in with iron ladles, so as to occupy every vacant space. The heavier part of the cement naturally fell to the bottom, while the fluid was absorbed by the stone. The vacancy thus left at the top was repeatedly re-filled, until all remained solid; then the top was pointed, and, where necessary, defended by a layer of plaster.

The whole of the foundation having thus been brought to a proper level, some other means were required to secure a similar degree of solidity for the superstructure.

A hole, one foot square, was accordingly cut right through the middle of the central stone in the sixth course; and at equal distances in the circumference were sunk eight other sockets, each one foot square, and six inches deep. A strong plug of hard marble, also one foot square, but twenty-two inches long, was driven into the aforementioned central cavity, and set fast with mortar and wedges. This course, however, was only thirteen inches in depth; consequently the marble plug rose nine inches above the surface.

Upon the block thus prepared was set the central stone of the next course, having a similar hole in the middle, so as to receive the upper portion of the marble plug. Hence it is clear that no force or pressure of the sea, acting horizontally on any one of these central stones, could move it from its position, unless it were able to cut in two the marble plug. To prevent the upper stone from being lifted, in case its mortar was destroyed, it was fixed down by four trenails. The blocks surrounding the central were dove-tailed together as before; and thus one course rose above another without any inter-ruption, except from the occasional inrush of the waves or violence of the weather.

Throughout this process, if there was any position of danger his men hesitated to occupy, Smeaton didn't hesitate to step forward and take the lead. One morning in the sum-mer of 1757, for example, when heaving up the moorings of the store-ship, preparatory to starting for the rock, the links of the buoy chain were exposed to a considerable strain. The davit-roll, which was only made of cast-iron, began to bend upon its convex surface. To remedy this, Smeaton ordered the carpenter to cut some trenails into small pieces, and split each length into two. He then had them fixed between the chain and the roll at the flexure of each link, so as to relieve the strain. One of the men remarked that if the chain should break anywhere between the roll and the tackle, the person who was inserting the wooden wedges would be cut in two by the chain, or carried overboard along with it. Smeaton, who never required others to do anything that he would not do himself, immediately ordered aside his men, took the "post of honor," as he called it, and superintended the getting in of the chain, link by link, until it was all on board.

In his superintendence of the difficult and laborious work, Smeaton's activity and perseverance were unwearied. As soon as it had been so far accomplished as to present the appearance of a level platform, he could not resist the pleasure of walking on it. But making a false step he fell over the edge of the masonry, and on to the rocks on the west side. As it was low water at the time, he received no serious injury. He dislocated his thumb, however, and as medical assistance was not available, he set it himself, afterwards returning to his work. This was the kind of firmness and resolution that Smeaton exhibited throughout his busy career.

The ninth course was laid on the 30th of September, and concluded the operations for the year.

But living in plymouth during the off season was not easy for Smeaton—not with his lighthouse still unfinished. We borrow the following sketch from Mr. Smiles:

"While living at Plymouth," he says, "the restless, enthusiastic engineer was accustomed every morning to take his post on the grassy summit of the Hoe, and with his telescope to survey the famous rock.

"The Hoe is an elevated promenade, occupying a high ridge of land between Mill Bay and the entrance to the harbor, with the citadel at its eastern extremity. It forms the seaport of Plymouth, and commands the beautiful and varied scenery of the Sound. In front of it lies St Nicholas's Island, bristling with fortifications; beyond, rising in verdurous slopes and terraces from the water's edge, is Mount Edg-cumbe Park, with its masses of luxuriant foliage backed by green hills.

"The land juts out on either side of the bay in rocky points, which are crowned with forts and batteries. While in the distance now, though not in Smeaton's time, there extends the nobly massive rampart of the breakwater, midway between the bluffs of Redding and Staddon Points, so as to arrest the long roll of the Atlantic waves and protect the placid expanse of the great harbor.

"It was from the Hoe that our ancestors first spied the immense array of the Spanish Armada advancing threateningly toward the English coast. It was the favorite watchtower, so to speak, of Sir Francis Drake in those times of difficulty and peril, as it was now of Smeaton in less critical circumstances. It may be added that these two men, each so illustrious in his special way, possessed many characteristic qualities in common. Perseverance, patience, heroic endurance, indomitable resolution; all of the qualities, in fact, by which great deeds are accomplished.

"Smeaton, when he ascended the Hoe after a stormy night at sea, had neither eye nor thought for the picturesque beauties or historical associations of the scene before him. All he could think of was his lighthouse on the rock. He knew that he had brought the fullest resources of skill, care, and planning to bear upon its erection, yet he could not avoid a feeling of anxiety as to the security of the foundation.

"There were many who still went about asserting that no fabric of stone could possibly stand upon the wave-worn, wind-beaten rock; and again and again the engineer, in the first dim light of morning, came to see if their ill-omened predictions had been fulfilled. Sometimes he had to wait long, until he could see a tall white column of spray rise aloft into the morning air. Then he breathed freely, shut his telescope, and thanked God that his labor had not been undone. And as the morning advanced, and the light grew fuller and stronger, he was able to discern his shapely light-tower, standing, erect and firm, above the whirl of waters."

* * *

On the 12th of May 1758, Smeaton and his "merry men" returned to the lonely wave-washed rock, and were delighted to find their work intact. The cement seemed to have become as hard as the stone itself, from which, indeed, it was scarcely distinguishable.

Lusty arms and willing hearts made rapid progress; and by September, the twenty-fourth course was reached and laid. It completed the "solid" part of the building, and was designed to form the floor of the store-room; so that Smeaton had good reason to be satisfied with the progress made. But he knew how great an advantage it would be to exhibit a light in the coming winter; and therefore he resolved on completing the storeroom, if within the range of the possible, and planting a light above it.

The building had hitherto been carried up as a solid mass of masonry, like a breakwater or seawall, to a height of 35 feet 4 inches above its base, and 27 feet above the summit of the rock. It was now reduced to 16 feet in diameter. Of this limited space it was needful to make good use, so far as was consistent with the primary and indispensable condition of strength.

The rooms were built with a diameter of 12 feet 4 inches, the walls being 2 feet 2 inches thick. These walls were built up of single blocks, and so shaped that a complete circle was formed by sixteen pieces, which were bound together with strong iron clamps, and secured to the lower courses by marble plugs in the fashion already described. That no damp might make its way through the vertical joints, flat stones were introduced into each, in such a manner as to be lodged partly in one block and partly in another. With all these careful and ingenious contrivances, the twenty-eighth course was completely set by the 30th of September.

This and the next course received the vaulted flooring, which answered the double purpose of the ceiling of the lower and the floor of the upper store-rooms. For additional security, a deep groove was here cut into the outer surface of the course, in which a massive iron chain was embedded in molten lead. The next course was laid and set after the same pattern; and by the 10th of October Smeaton had nearly completed his arrangements for establishing a light and light-keepers at the Eddystone, when they were interrupted by legal difficulties, which had arisen between the lessee of the rock and the Trinity House Corporation.

These were not settled until the following year, so that Smeaton was unable to resume operations before the 5th of July. He worked, however, with so much vigor that the second stage was finished by the 21st; and on the 29th the fortieth course was set, and the third floor finished.

The main column, or body, of the lighthouse was completed on the 17th of August, consisting of forty-six courses of masonry, and attaining an elevation of 70 feet. The last work done was singularly appropriate: the masons carved the words "Laus Deo" (Praise be to God!) on the last stone set above the lantern.

All honest work should thus be dedicated to Him through whose infinite goodness we are permitted to achieve it. At an earlier date, Smeaton, in devout recognition of the Eternal Power, had inscribed on the course of masonry beneath the ceiling of the upper store-room, "Except the Lord build the house, they labor in vain that build it" It was in this spirit that the great engineer entered upon and accomplished his wonderful enterprises; and it is in this spirit that each of us should go through our daily toil, as if feeling ourselves ever in the immediate presence of our Father, and knowing that we strive, and endure, and hope, and suffer before his all-seeing eye.

The iron-work of the balcony and lantern were next erected, and the gracefully strong and massive structure was crowned by a gilded ball.

The interior of Smeaton's lighthouse was (and is) arranged as follows:

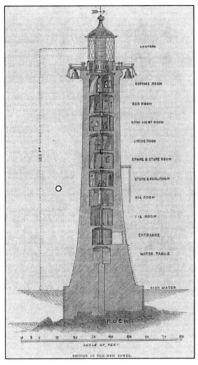

The Various levels of Smeaton's Eddystone Lighthouse

On the ground-floor: Store-room, with a doorway, but no windows.

First stage, or story: Upper store-room, with two loopholed-windows.

Second stage: Kitchen, with fire-place and sink; two settles, with lockers; a dresser, with drawers; two cupboards; and a rack for dishes, Four windows.

Third stage: Bedroom, with three cabin-beds, each large enough for an adult; three drawers, and two lockers in each, to receive the clothing and other property of the light-keepers. Four windows.

Fourth: Lantern, with circular bench, or seat.

In fixing the window-bars, Smeaton met with an accident which might easily have been attended with fatal results. He thus describes the circumstances:

"After the boat was gone, and it became so dark that we could not see any longer to pursue our occupations, I ordered a charcoal-fire to be made in the upper store-room, in one of the iron pots we used for melting lead, for the purpose of annealing the blank ends of the bars; and they were made hot all together in the charcoal. Most of the workmen were set round the fire; and by way of making ourselves comfortable, by screening ourselves and the fire from the wind, the windows were shut, and, as well as I remember, the copper cover or hatch put over the man-hole of the floor of the room where the fire was—the hatch above being left open for the heated vapor to ascend. I remember to have looked into the fire attentively to see that the iron was made hot enough, but not overheated. I also remember I felt my head a very little giddy; but the next thing of which I had any sensation or idea was finding myself upon the floor of the room below, half drowned with water. It seems that, without being further sensible of anything to give me warning, the effluvia of the charcoal so suddenly overcame all sensation, that I dropped down upon the floor; and had not the people hauled me down to the room below, where they did not spare for cold water to throw in my face and upon me, I certainly should have expired upon the spot."

Smeaton, however, was saved for future useful service; and on the 16th of October the welcome light shone once more from the dreaded Eddystone Rock. Storm-tossed mariners have depended on it ever since.

On entering the English Channel from the west and south, the cautious navigator feels his way by careful soundings on the great bank which extends from the Channel into the Atlantic. These are repeated at fixed intervals until land is in sight. Every fathom nearer shore increases a ship's risks, especially in nights when, to use the seaman's phrase, it is 'as dark as a pocket.'

The men are on the lookout, peering anxiously into the dark, straining the eye to catch the glimmer of a light; and when it is known that 'the Eddystone is in sight,' a thrill runs through the ship. It is something that can only be appreciated by those who have felt or witnessed it after long months of weary voyaging. Its gleam across the waters has thus been a source of joy, and given a sense of relief to thousands. For the beaming of a clear light from one known and fixed spot is infallible in its truthfulness, and a safer guide for the seaman than the bearings of many hazy and ill-defined headlands."

Occasionally a strong wave will strike full upon it, and the

Smeaton's Eddystone Light as it appears today on the Hoe, in Plymouth England.

wave, swiftly gliding up the perpendicular shaft, leaps with one tremendous bound over the lantern. At other times, a billow will break against it with a fury which seems to menace the security of its foundation. To those within, the report is like that of heavy artillery, and the windows rattle, and the whole building quivers from top to base. But the keepers know that the shudder which then runs throughout the lighthouse, instead of being a sign of weakness, is the "strongest proof of the unity and close connection of the fabric in all its parts."

For more than a century the Eddystone light has withstood the storm, an enduring monument to the fame of its great architect

CHAPTER FIVE
Smeaton in Later Life

We find little record of Smeaton's life between 1759, when he completed his great undertaking, and 1764, when he applied for and obtained the appointment of receiver for the Derwentwater Estates.[1] It may be, as one of his biographers remarks, that, as yet, there was little demand in England for the skill of so bold and able an engineer.

Not that there wasn't work to be done. The highways were in a deplorable condition; and, in many districts, travel was rendered difficult by the lack of adequate bridges. In the commercial ports of the country proper dock accommodation was almost unknown. But England was then too poor, or her energies were too exclusively concentrated upon maritime enterprise and colonial extension, for her to undertake to supply these deficiencies on any extensive scale.

Smeaton's reputation, however, was gradually extending throughout the kingdom, and in 1760 we find him consulted

---

[1] These estates were confiscated by the Crown, on the death of the last Earl of Derwentwater—executed for high treason, and conferred by Parliament on Greenwich Hospital

by the magistrates of Dumfries respecting the improvement of the river Nith. He was similarly consulted as to the lockage of the river Wear, the opening up of the navigation of the Chelmer to Chelmsford, of the Don above Doncaster, of the Devon in Clackmannanshire, of the Tetney Haven navigation near Louth, and the improvement of the river Lea. But the improvements he recommended do not seem to have been carried out, because of lack of funds.

In truth, his first great engineering enterprise was undertaken in his home county, where he was employed in extensive repairs of the dams and locks on the river Calder. He effected many important improvements in that river, which confirmed the general belief in his skill and judgment. At the same time he carried out extensive works on the river Aire from Leeds to its junction with the Ouse.

Smeaton is also credited with the recovery of the inundated lands in the Lincoln Fens, and in the low areas between Doncaster and Hull. The river Witham, between Lincoln and Boston, was still, it is said, a source of constant grief and loss to the farmers along its banks. It had become choked up by neglect, so that "not only had the navigation of the river become almost lost, but a large extent of otherwise valuable land was constantly laid under water."

At a still later period he undertook to improve the drainage of the North Level of the Fens, and the outfall of the Nene at Wisbeach. For this purpose he recommended the construction of a powerful outfall-sluice at the mouth of the Nene.

Other works in which he was consulted, and in which his engineering ability was signally manifested, may here be mentioned: the drainage of the lands adjacent to the river Went, in Yorkshire; of the Earl of Kinnoul's lands lying along the Almond and the Tay, in Perthshire; the Adling Fleet Level, at the junction of the Ouse and the Trent; Hotham Carrs, near Market-Weighton; the Lewes Laughton Level, in Sussex; the Potterick Carr Fen, near Doncaster; the Torksey

Bridge Fen, near Gainsborough; and the Holderness Level, near Hull.

In 1763, he was called upon by the Corporation of London to advise them as to the best means of improving, widening, and enlarging Old London Bridge. In order to accommodate the increased traffic on the river, two arches of the bridge had been combined into one. The problem was that this channeled the rush of the water so as to loosen the adjoining piers by washing away the bed of the river under their foundations. The alarm was so great that few persons would pass either over or under the bridge; and the Corporation hastily summoned Smeaton, who was then in Yorkshire, to their assistance.

On his arrival, he proceeded immediately to examine the bridge, and to sound the foundations of the piers as minutely as possible. He then advised the Corporation to repurchase the stones of the city gates, which had recently been taken down and their material sold, and cast them into the river outside the startings, or buttresses of the piers, to protect them from the action of the tide. His advice was adopted; and simple as were the means suggested, they proved entirely effective.

This method of checking the impetuous ravages of water, says Holmes, he had practiced before with success on the river Calder. "On my calling on him in the neighborhood of Wakefield, he showed me the effects of a great flood, which had made a considerable passage over the land; this he stopped at the bank of the river, by throwing in a quantity of large, rough stones, which, with the sand and other materials washed down by the river, filling up their interstices, had become a barrier to keep the river in its usual course."

Smeaton next appears in the character of a bridge-builder. The handsome bridges at Perth, Coldstream, and Banff were erected by him.

With reference to the first of these, it should be explained that the Tay being subject to frequent flooding, it was important that great care should be taken with the foundations, which were laid down by means of coffer-dams. That is, a row of piles was driven into the river-bed, and round about and between them was thrown a quantity of gravel and earth mixed together, so as to render the enclosed space impervious to water. Pumping power was then applied, and the bed of the river within the coffer-dam was laid completely dry; after which the soil was excavated to a proper depth, and a firm foundation obtained for the piles. Piles were driven into

St. Matthew's Church and Smeaton's Bridge, in Perth, Scotland.
*(Source: "Perth, Scotland." Wikipedia, The Free Encyclopedia.
7 Mar 2008, 16:01 UTC. Wikimedia Foundation, Inc.)*

the earth underneath the intended foundation-frame, and then the building was carried upwards in the usual way.

The Perth bridge is a handsome structure, consisting of seven principal arches, and measures about nine hundred feet in length. It was completed and opened for traffic in 1772.

His success in this notable undertaking secured him a considerable amount of engineering business in the North. At Edinburgh he found employment in improving the water-supply for that city; at Glasgow, in strengthening and securing the old bridge. Far more important were the works he executed in designing and constructing the Forth and Clyde Canal, which links together the east and west coasts of Scotland, the North Sea and the Irish Sea.

After a careful examination of the various lines which had been proposed for the canal, Smeaton strongly recommended the adoption of the most direct route possible, and suggested that the depth of the canal should be sufficient to accommodate vessels of large burden. Lord Dundas, the principal promoter of the scheme, adopted Smeaton's ideas, and took the necessary steps for obtaining an Act to authorize the construction of the Forth and Clyde Canal, which was accordingly commenced in 1768.

The Forth and Clyde Canal within Glasgow, showing Ruchill Church. *(Source: "Forth and Clyde Canal." Wikipedia, The Free Encyclopedia. 17 Dec 2007, Wikimedia Foundation, Inc.)*

This canal runs nearly parallel with the famous wall of Antoninus, erected by the Romans to protect the southern Lowlands from the predatory attacks of the wild tribes of Caledonia. It begins at a point near Grangemouth, on the Forth, and ends at Bowling, on the Clyde, a few miles below

Glasgow. Its length is about 38 miles, and it includes 39 locks, with an elevation of 156 feet from the sea to the summit-level.

It was one of the most difficult works, we are told, which, up to that time, had been constructed in Great Britain, The engineer's resources were severely tested by the occurrence of rocks and quicksands. In some places the canal was carried over deep rivers, in others along embankments exceeding twenty feet in height It traverses numerous roads and scores of rivulets; besides the streams of the Luggie (celebrated by the peasant-poet David Gray), and the Kelvin (immortalized by Burns). The bridge over the latter is 275 feet long and 68 feet high. The depth of the canal averages 8 feet. The total cost of the undertaking did not amount to £200,000.

Smeaton's next engagement was to construct a bridge across the Tweed at Coldstream. It consists of five principal arches, of which the central has a span of 60 feet 8 inches; the two lateral, of 60 feet 5 inches each; and the two land or side arches, 58 feet. It was completed at a total cost of about £6000; and opened in October 1766, having been upwards of three years in building. It will serve to show the great advance that has been made in engineering science since the days of Smeaton, when we state that a similar bridge could now be erected in nine months; though, owing to the rise in wages and in the price of materials, at a much greater cost.

Smeaton also furnished the design for the bridge over the river Deveron, near Banff, in Scotland It consists of seven arches, segments of circles, and measures 410 feet in length, and 20 feet in width. It resembles, in its leading features, the bridge at Perth; and its simple yet graceful aspect, added to the exceeding beauty of its position, renders it a much-admired object, and one of great pictorial interest.

Smeaton built only one bridge in England, and, strange to say, it was his only failure. He was requested, in 1777, to furnish a design for a bridge to be erected across the Tyne at

Hexham; and a very handsome structure, of nine arches, it proved to be. But it had scarcely been finished before a subsidence took place in the foundation of one of the piers; and an attempt was made to remedy the defect by "sheet-piling," and by filling up the cavities in the river's bed with rough rubble-stones.

In the spring of 1782, however, a sudden violent flood swept down the river, and in the course of a few hours the beautiful Hexham Bridge lay in ruin at the bottom of the Tyne. Writing to his engineer, he said: "All our honors are now in the dust! It cannot now be said that in the course of thirty years practice, and [after being] engaged in some of the most difficult enterprises, not one of Smeaton's works has failed! Hexham Bridge is a melancholy instance to the contrary... The news came to me like a thunderbolt, as it was a stroke I least expected, and even yet can scarcely form a practical belief as to its reality. There is, however, one consolation that attends this great misfortune; and that is, that I cannot see that anybody is really to blame, or that anybody is blamed, as we all did our best, according to what appeared; and all the experience I have gained is not to attempt to build a bridge upon a gravel bottom in a river subject to such violent rapidity."

Among his various engineering enterprises, Smeaton was employed in the improvement and construction of various harbors.

His first work of this kind was at St. Ives, in Cornwall. Here he received much help from nature, which had provided a well-sheltered bay-enclosed between two elevated headlands, known as the Island and Penower Point, respectively. Thus it was protected from the winds of the north, west, and south, and from the prevalent storms from the southwest, which beat with so much violence on the iron-bound Cornish coast. All that Smeaton, therefore, had to do, was to afford security for shipping from gales rising in the east and northeast; and this he effected by constructing a pier running nearly south from the southern angle of the Island. The port thus formed has proved of great advantage to the town, which is now one of the principal seats of the pilchard fishery, and the emporium of a busy mining district

Smeaton's skill was also called into service for many other harbors: Whitehaven, Workington, and Bristol, on the west coast; Rye, Christ-church, and Dover, on the south; and Yarmouth, Lynn, Scarborough, and Sunderland, on the east

His principal work in harbor-construction, however, was that which he accomplished at Ramsgate.

"The proximity of this harbor to the Downs," says Mr. Smiles, "and to the month of the Thames, rendered it of considerable importance; and its improvement for purposes of trade, as well as for the shelter of distressed vessels in stormy weather, was long regarded as a matter of almost national importance.

The neighborhood of Sandwich was first proposed for a harbor of refuge as early as the reign of Queen Elizabeth, and the subject was revived in succeeding reigns. In 1737, Labelye, the architect of [old] Westminster Bridge, was called upon to investigate the subject. Ten years later, a committee of the House of Commons, after taking full evidence and obtaining every information, reported that 'a safe and commodious harbor may be made into the Downs near Sandown Castle, fit for the reception and security of large merchantmen and ships of war, which would also be of great advantage to the naval power of Great Britain.'

The estimated cost of the proposed harbor was, however, considered too formidable, although it was under half a million; and the project lay dormant until a violent storm occurred in the Downs in 1748, by which a great number of ships were forced from their anchors and driven on shore. Several vessels, however, found safety in the little haven at Ramsgate, which was then only used by fishermen, the whole extent of its harbor accommodation consisting merely of a rough rubble-pier."

It would seem that this circumstance once more directed

the attention of the public to Ramsgate as a suitable site for a harbor of refuge for vessels caught in a gale in the Downs.

Petitions on the subject were addressed to the House of Commons, and the Government taking it up, an Act was passed in 1749 authorizing the construction of a harbor at Ramsgate.

The trustees invited plans from various individuals, and from these selected a curious combination; adopting the west pier of one of the amateur engineers, and the east pier of another, the former to be of stone, and the latter of timber. The east pier was designed by a trustee; the west, by a ship-captain resident at Margate.

While the works, thus strangely designed, were in progress, the Harbor Trustees proposed to reduce their area, and consequently the accommodation to be afforded to shipping. As soon as their intention became known, the shipping interest memorialized Parliament against it. In 1755 an inspection of the works was ordered, and led to their suspension, nor were they again resumed for a period of fully six years, during which the Government officials and the Harbor Trustees carried on a war of words. When they were once more set on foot, they proved eminently unsatisfactory, so far as their object was concerned, the protection of shipping; large quantities of sand and silt rapidly collecting in the harbor, and threatening to choke it up altogether.

This awkward circumstance induced the Harbor Board, in 1770, to call Mr. Smeaton to their councils. After a careful examination, he ascertained that no fewer than 268,700 cubic yards of sand and mud had already silted up, every tide bringing in a fresh quantity and depositing it in the tranquil water of the harbor, which possessed no natural scour to carry it away.

In order to create such a scour, Smeaton proposed the construction of an adequate number of sluices, fed by an artificial backwater. He showed that Ramsgate harbor, having a sound bottom of chalk, was excellently adapted to insure the success of such a scheme; and pointed out that if the silt could thus be set in motion, the tide, running diagonally upon the harbor mouth, would easily carry it away.

The proposition of our engineer, in detail, was as follows:

To enclose two spaces of four acres each, provided with nine draw-gates: namely, four upon the westernmost, and five upon the easternmost basin, the whole pointing in three different directions; two towards the curve of the west pier, four towards the harbor mouth, and three towards the curve in the east pier.

To give the sluices all possible effect, he recommended the construction of a caisson, shaped somewhat like the pier of a bridge, which, being floated to its place, and then sunk, might serve to direct the current right or left, according to circumstances.

After some discussion, the trustees resolved to adopt Smeaton's plan; but as it was not carried out in strict accordance with his intentions, another failure occurred, necessitating a recourse for the second time to his advice.

Among the improvements which he now recommended was the construction of a new dock, the first stone of which was laid in July 1784. In the course of the excavations numerous springs were tapped and for these, breaking through the pavement with which the dock had been laid, Portland stone was substituted, in blocks of considerable size. These, too, proved of no avail, and Smeaton was again sent for, with the result that the execution of all further works connected with the harbor was put into his hands. The dock was rebuilt; a timber floor was laid throughout in the most complete manner possible. An additional thickness was given to the walls; the east pier was rebuilt of stone, and carried out into deep water to a further extent of 350 feet.

In constructing this extension, Smeaton first employed the diving-bell in building the foundations, employing a square iron chest, weighing about half a ton. It measured four feet six inches in height and length, and three feet in width. Two men could work together in its interior, and these were supplied with a constant current of fresh air by means of a forcing-pump placed in a boat which floated above them.

The works, when finished, proved successful, and Ramsgate harbor still remains the best upon the southeast coast, affording a refuge in stormy weather to vessels of considerable draught of water. It includes an area of forty-two acres; the piers extending 310 feet into the sea, with an opening between the pier-heads of 200 feet in width. The inner basin serves the purpose of a wet dock, and there is also a dry dock in which skips can be repaired. A lighthouse has been erected on the east pier. In the season, when Ramsgate is crowded with visitors, the two piers afford ample opportunities for promenading, and present a scene of much liveliness and interest, which is enhanced by the numerous vessels at anchor in the basin, and by a picturesque background of chalky cliffs and grassy hills and shining sands.

In addition to his numerous works on the English coast, Smeaton was largely employed in Scotland, in inspecting the harbors there, and devising schemes for increasing their security and amount of accommodation.

We learn from Mr. Smiles that in 1770 the harbor at Aberdeen was altered in accordance with his suggestions; and a great depth of water was obtained over the bar at its mouth, as well as in the channel of the river Dee, by the erection of a north pier, and other additions. Improvements were also carried out at Dundee and Dunbar under his superintendence.

He constructed the small harbors at Portpatrick on the west, and Eyemouth on the east coast "Both of these," says our authority, "were in a great measure formed by nature, and the improvement of them demanded comparatively small skill on the part of the engineer. He had merely to follow the direction of the rocks, which provided a natural foundation for his piers at both places.

Of his little harbor at Eyemouth he was somewhat proud,

as it was one of the first he constructed, and very effectually answered its purpose at a comparatively small outlay of money. It lies at the corner of a bay, opposite St. Abb's Head, on the coast of Berwickshire, and is almost landlocked, excepting from the north, Smeaton accordingly carried his north pier into deep water, for the purpose of protecting the harbor's mouth from that quarter, as well as enlarging the accommodation of the haven. The harbor was thus rendered perfectly safe in all winds, and proved of great convenience and safety to the fishing-craft by which it is chiefly frequented."

It is to be observed that Smeaton, unlike some of our modern engineers, was very solicitous to do his work economically, and that he always contented himself with recommending such improvements or modifications as would answer the desired purpose, without seeking to gain a brilliant reputation by ambitious and costly schemes.

These details, of bridges and harbors, and piers and sluice-gates, may not be interesting to the reader, but they are valuable as illustrations of the credit which Smeaton enjoyed as a successful and capable engineer, and of his restless industry and indefatigable perseverance. He crowded an extraordinary amount of good and useful achievement into his active life, and whatever he did was done so carefully and conscientiously as never to require patching or re-doing.

In the course of his engineering labors he traversed Great Britain from north to south, and east to west; and there was scarcely a bridge or a canal in the kingdom which he did not restore, enlarge, or in some way improve.

As might be expected, he remained, throughout his life, the great authority on all questions connected with lighthouses. He erected those which on Spurn Head still guard the mouth of the Humber, and at other parts of the coast his services were called into requisition to secure their improved lightage.

He was also consulted by Government respecting the national dockyards at Portsmouth and Plymouth. When a new water company was started to supply some hitherto unprovided town or district, or when an old company found it necessary to afford increased accommodation, recourse was had to the inexhaustible skill and ingenuity of Smeaton, who for a considerable period was really consulting engineer to the nation.

He was called upon to advise the landowner who wished to drain his estates, and the coal-owner who desired to work his mines more safely and efficiently. There seems to have been no department of engineering science in which he was not largely and successfully employed.

It is said of him, and without exaggeration, that he was ready to supply a design of any new machine, from a fire-bucket or a ship's pump to a turning-lathe or a steam-engine. His genius was equally at home with small things as with great. Whatever he designed was remarkable for the finish and neatness of its execution.

"The water-pumping engine which he erected for Lord Irwin, at Temple-Newsham, near his own house at Austhorpe, to pump the water for the supply of the mansion, is an admirable piece of workmanship, and continues at this day in good working condition.

His advice was especially sought on subjects connected with mill-work, water-pumping, and engineering of every description—flour-mills and powder-mills, wind-mills and water-mills, fulling-mills and flint-mills, blade-mills and forge-hammer mills. From a list left by him in his own handwriting, it appears that he designed and erected forty-three water-mills of various kinds, besides numerous wind-mills. Water-power was then used for nearly all purposes for which steam is now applied, such as grinding flour, sawing wood, boring and hammering iron, fulling cloth, rolling copper, and driving all kinds of machinery."

Smeaton also bestowed much attention on the development of the wonderful powers of the steam-engine, then only in its infancy. In order to experiment with it, he erected a model engine, on Newcomen's principle, near his house at Austhorpe. And his fertile genius soon devised a variety of improvements which added to its utility. His Chacewater engine of 150 horsepower was looked upon as the finest and most powerful of its kind which had until then been erected.

In this field of invention, however, it must be admitted that he was completely surpassed by James Watt, the superior merit of whose condensing engine—notwithstanding the time and labor Smeaton had bestowed on the development of Newcomen's—he frankly acknowledged. After inspecting Watt's engine, he said at once: "That the old engine, even when made to do its best, was now driven from every place where fuel could be considered of any value."

During many years the opinion of Smeaton was considered of so much authority, that no engineering works of any importance were undertaken throughout the kingdom except on his advice, or under his superintendence. He was constantly consulted in Parliament, and was regarded as an arbiter or ultimate referee on all difficult questions connected with his profession,

And it should be added, for the benefit of the young reader, that he was never in a hurry to give his opinion; and that he never gave it until he had made himself thoroughly acquainted with the subject on which it was sought. He was above all petty artifices, and never laid claim to the possession of universal knowledge. He did not pretend to be able to decide off-hand on a question he had not considered, but studied it thoroughly and patiently before he ventured to offer an opinion. Hence it was always received with the utmost deference, and the most implicit confidence was placed in his proved integrity.

Smeaton possessed the gift of fluent and clear description. He could make difficult points of engineering science intelligible even to non-professional readers or hearers; and in the courts of law he Was frequently complimented by Lord

Mansfield and the other judges for the light he so ingeniously threw upon abstruse and very difficult subjects. His secret was, his thorough knowledge of what he wrote or spoke about. He was always thorough, and hence he always spoke with the decision and confidence of a master. It is only imperfect knowledge which forever blunders into obscurity.

CHAPTER SIX
Smeaton's last years

WHILE Smeaton was thus reaping the reward of his diligent life and conscientious industry, he continued to make his home and resting-place at Austhorpe, near Leeds, where he had been born. There he carried on the mechanical experiments in which he had ever felt so intense a delight.

His father had allowed him the privilege of a workshop in an outhouse, and he occupied it for many years. Afterwards, when the house had become his settled residence, he erected a workshop, a study, and an observatory, all in one, for his own use. This building assumed the form of a square tower, four stories high. It stood apart from the house, on the opposite side of the court or green, and on the bank of a pleasant pool. Shrouded in ivy, and embowered among trees, it now forms a picturesque feature in the landscape.

The ground-floor was devoted to his forge; the first floor contained his lathe; the second, his models; the third, his study; while the fourth was a sort of lumber-room and attic. From the little turreted staircase on the top a door opened upon the leads. A vane was fixed on the summit, and so arranged that it set in motion the hands of a dial on the ceiling of his drawing-room, and showed at any moment the precise direction in which the wind blew.

As soon as the engineer retired to his study, strict orders were issued that he was not to be disturbed on any account. No person was suffered to ascend the circular staircase which led to his retreat. If he heard a step below, he would immediately raise his voice to know the intruder's business. Even his smith, Waddington, was prohibited from trespassing on the sanctuary, and required, on such occasions, to wait in the lower apartment until Mr. Smeaton came down.

When he was neither evolving plans nor drawing up reports, Smeaton delighted to occupy his leisure with astronomical studies and observations; and this scientific pastime he continued to indulge in even in the flush of his prosperous professional career, when he was the consulting engineer of all England. For many years he regularly contributed papers on astronomical subjects to the Royal Society, of which he was a Fellow. The instruments he used in making his observations were all of his own workmanship, and remarkable for their accuracy and finish.

His contrivances of tools, we are told, were endless, and he was constantly employed in inventing and making new ones. Of these interesting relics large quantities are still, says Smiles, in the possession of the son of his blacksmith, who lives in the neighborhood of Austhorpe. When Mr. Smiles made inquiry after them, they were found lying in a heap in an open shed, begrimed and rusty.

One mysterious article, after it had been thoroughly scrubbed and cleansed, proved to be a jack-plane, and the tool which Smeaton himself had handled. His drill was also found, the bow being formed of a thick piece of cane; his brace, his T square, his augers, his gouges, and his engraving tools.

"There was no end of curiously arranged dividers; pulleys in large numbers, and of various sizes; cog-wheels, brass hemispheres, and all manner of measured, drilled, framed, and jointed brass-work. These remains of the great engineer are worthy of preservation. To mechanics, there is a meaning in every one of them. They do not resemble existing tools, but you can see at once that each was made for a reason; and one can almost detect what the contriver was thinking about when he made them so different from those we are accustomed to see. Even in the most trifling matters, such as the kind of wood or metal used, and the direction of the fiber of the wood, each detail has been carefully studied.

Much of the household furniture seems to have been employed in their fabrication, possibly to the occasional amazement of the ladies in Smeaton's house over the way. We are informed that so much 'rubbish,' as it was termed, was found in that square tower at his death, that a fire was kindled in the yard, and a vast quantity of papers, letters, books, plans, tools, and scraps of all kinds, were remorselessly burnt."

There can be no question that Smeaton was "a born mechanic;" and to the end of his days a mechanic he remained, finding his greatest pleasure in mechanical pursuits. It is told of him that when new gates were erected at the entrances to Temple-Newsham Park, near his house at Austhorpe, he offered to supply the design; and they were accordingly constructed and hung after his plans.

In the popular opinion, however, his noblest work, surpassing even the Eddystone lighthouse, is the ingenious hydraulic ram, by means of which the water is still raised in the beautiful grounds of Temple-Newsham.

Occasionally he diversified his occupations in his workshop, and at his desk, by visits to his smithy. Here he was wont to experiment upon a boiler, the lower part of copper and the upper of lead, which he had fitted up in an adjacent building, for the purpose of ascertaining the evaporative power of different kinds of fuel, and of settling other questions connected with the all-absorbing subject of steam-power.

He was on the best of terms with his smith, and if he thought him not very dexterous in the execution of any particular piece of work, he would take the tools himself, and show him how it ought to be done. He was fond of repeating the maxim, "Never let a file come where a hammer can go."

When superintending the various works on which he was successively employed, if any workman showed a lack of skill, or seemed unable to proceed, he would at once take his tools and finish the task himself.

"You know, sir," said the son of Smeaton's blacksmith to an inquirer, "workmen didn't know much about drawings at that time a-day, and so when Mr. Smeaton wanted any queer-fangled thing making, he'd cut one piece out of wood, and say to my father, 'Now, lad, go make me this,' and so on forever so many pieces; and then he'd stick all those pieces o' wood together, and say, 'Now, lad, thou knows how thou made each part, go make it now all in a piece.' And I've heard my father say 'at he's often been cap't to know how he could tell so soon when owt ailed it; for before ever he set his foot at t' bottom of his twisting steps, or before my father could get sight of his face, if t' iron had been wrong, thear'd been an angry word o' some sort, but t' varry next words were, 'Why, my lad, thou o'ud a' made it so and so: now go make another.' "

It is related by his daughter, Mrs. Dickson, that early in life Smeaton attracted the notice of the eccentric Duke and Duchess of Queensberry, owing to the remarkable personal likeness between him and their favorite Gay, the poet.

Their first acquaintance was made under sufficiently singular circumstances.

When the engineer, one night, was walking in Ranelagh Gardens, then a fashionable place of resort, with Mrs. Smeaton, he observed an elderly-lady and gentleman fixing their eyes upon him with a persistent gaze. At last they stopped, and the Duchess said, "Sir, I don't know who you are, or what you are, but so strongly do you resemble my poor dear

Gay that we must be acquainted. You shall go home and sup with us; and if the minds of the two men accord as do the countenances, you will find two cheerful old folks who can love you well; and I think (or you are a hypocrite), you can as well deserve it."

The invitation thus frankly given was as frankly accepted, and proved the beginning of a friendship which continued cordial and uninterrupted so long as the Duke and Duchess lived.

During Smeaton's visits a game at cards was sometimes proposed Smeaton, however, disliked cards, and could never devote his attention to the game. On one occasion the stakes were already high, and it fell to Smeaton's lot to double them, when, neglecting to deal the cards, he appeared to be busily engaged in making some abstruse calculations on paper, which he placed upon the table. The Duchess asked eagerly what they referred to. Smeaton calmly replied, "You will recollect that the field in which my house stands measures about five acres three roods and seven perches, which, at thirty years' purchase, will be just my stake; and if your grace will make a duke of me, I presume the winner will not dislike my mortgage." The jesting lesson had its effect, and they never played again, except for the veriest trifle.

Smeaton, on one occasion, obtained a public appointment for a clerk in whom he placed the greatest confidence, and, conjointly with a friend, became security for him to a considerable amount. Not long afterwards this man committed the crime of forgery, was detected, and given up to justice. "The same post," says Mrs. Dickson, "brought news of the melancholy transaction, of the man's compunction and danger, of the claim of the bond forfeited, and of the refusal of the other person to pay their share. Being present when he read his letters, which arrived at a period of Mrs. Smeaton's declining health, so entirely did the command of himself second his anxious attention to her, that no emotion was visible on their perusal; nor, until all was put into the best train possible, did a word or look betray the exquisite distress it occasioned him. In the interim all which could soothe the remorse of a prisoner, every means which could save (which did, at least, from public execution), were exerted for him, with a characteristic benevolence, active and unobtrusive."

Smeaton was a man of blameless character; his integrity was as pure as his energy was unresting. Though his opportunities of amassing wealth were numerous, he cared but little for them. Profit was always, with Smeaton, a secondary consideration; his first aim being to execute the task entrusted to him with all the skill at his command. He never slighted his work, but attended to its minutest details.

Many lucrative appointments were placed at his disposal. The Empress Catherine of Russia endeavored, by the most splendid offers, to secure his services for her own country; but Smeaton was too sincere a patriot to be dazzled by any bribe. "The disinterested moderation of his ambition," says his daughter, and says so truly, "every transaction in private life evinced; his public ones bore the same stamp; and after his health had withdrawn him from the labors of his profession, many instances may be given by those whose concerns induced them to press importunately for a resumption of it; and when some of them seemed disposed to enforce their entreaties by further prospects of lucrative recompense, his reply was strongly characteristic of his simple manners and moderation.

He introduced the old woman who took care of his chambers in Gray's Inn, and showing her, asserted that 'her attendance sufficed for all his wants.' The inference was indisputable, for money could not tempt that man to forego his ease, leisure, or independence, whose requisites of accommodation were compressed within such limits!"

A very high opinion of his probity, and independence was formed by all who had transactions with him. The Princess Daschkaw, on behalf of the Empress of Russia, used every persuasion and offered every inducement to accept the superintendence of the vast projects she had conceived for the development of the resources of her empire. When all her negotiations failed, she remarked: "Sir, you are a great man, and I honor you! You may have an equal in ability, perhaps, but in character you stand alone. The English premier, Sir Robert Walpole, was mistaken, and my sovereign has the misfortune to find one man who has not his price."

In all the social duties of life Smeaton was above praise; and he was quick to recognize and encourage real merit wherever he found it. To strangers his mode of expression might at times appear too warm and harsh; but this may be accounted for, perhaps, as Mr. Holmes accounts for it, by the intense application of his mind, which was always absorbed in the pursuit of truth, or engaged in extending the domains of human knowledge. Hence, if interrupted by anything not in accordance with the general current of his thoughts, he was apt to speak hastily. As a friend, he was sincere, earnest, generous; as a companion, interesting and entertaining, and his conversation was always fresh, happy, and suggestive.

In his own home, and by his family and dependants, he was equally beloved and revered. After his wife's death in 1784, his two daughters managed his household until his own departure. The elder has left on record many graphic particulars of his mode of life, and has drawn his character in terms dictated by affection, yet, as unquestionable evidence shows, without undue exaggeration.

Though communicative on most subjects, she says, and stored with ample and liberal observations on others, of himself he never spoke. In nothing does he seem to have stood more single than in being devoid of that egotism which more or less affects the world. It required some address, even in his family, to draw him into conversation directly relating to himself, his pursuits, or his success. Self-opinion, self-interest, and self-indulgence, seemed alike tempered in him by a modesty inseparable from merit; and by a moderation in pecuniary ambition, a habit of intense application, and a rigid temperance, which, however laudable, are certainly uncommon.

Devoted to his family with an affection so profound, a manner at once so cheerful and serene, that it is impossible to say whether the charm of conversation, the simplicity of instruction, or the gentleness with which it was conveyed, most endeared his home. It was a home in which, from their earliest years, his children could not recollect having seen in him a sign of dissatisfaction, or to have heard a word of asperity. Yet with all this he ruled his household, not his household him. He was the loving and generous father, but he was also the firm and resolved master. But it is for "casuistry, or education, or rule, to explain his authority; it was an authority as impossible to dispute as it is to define."

In person our engineer was of middle stature, broadly and strongly made, like most Yorkshire-men, and endowed with a constitution of great natural vigor. The expression of his countenance was marked by much gentleness and shrewdness. In his ordinary address he was plain, unpretending, simple, but never rude Or awkward He had the characteristic straightforwardness of speech of the north-countryman, and never hesitated to call a lie a lie, or to stigmatize an act of dishonesty or deception in the plainest possible terms. He spoke in the dialect of his native county, and had the good sense not to be ashamed of it. His incessant avocations prevented him from acquiring that polish and superficial refinement so much valued by little minds—excellent things in themselves, but dearly purchased at the cost of sterling qualities of head or heart. He was born an engineer, a son of toil; and such he remained to the last.

Towards the close of his life, Smeaton became an author; not, however, with a view to literary reputation, but in the hope he might do some service to those coming after him by an accurate account of the various important works in which he had been engaged as an engineer. He meditated several compilations of this character, but lived to complete only his "Narrative of the Construction of the Eddystone Lighthouse." He frankly tells us that he found the task of describing this structure far more difficult than that of raising it; and hence, like most unaccustomed writers, he became singularly impressed with a sense of the importance of literary composition.

"I am convinced," he says in his preface, "that to write a book tolerably well is not a light or an easy matter; for, as I have proceeded in this task, I have been less and less satisfied with the execution. In truth, I have found much more difficulty in writing than I did in building, as well as a greater length of time and application of mind to be employed I am indeed now older by thirty-five years than I was when I first entered on that enterprise, and therefore my faculties are less active and vigorous; but when I consider that I have been employed full seven years, at every opportunity, in forwarding this book, having all the original draughts and materials to go upon, and that the production of these original materials, as well as the building itself, were despatched in half that time, I am almost tempted to subscribe to the sentiment adopted by Mr. Pope, that

Nature's chief masterpiece is writing well.

It is true that I have not been bred to literature, but it is equally true that I was no more bred to mechanics: we must therefore conclude that the same mind has in reality a much greater facility in some subjects than in others."

We agree with Mr. Smiles, however, in thinking that Smeaton's story of the Eddystone Lighthouse is very effectively told. It is distinguished by its intense dramatic interest; an interest arising from the contest it depicts between the colossal forces of nature and human resolution, energy, and skill. It has been well observed by the Earl of Ellesmere, in his "Essays on Engineering," that bloody battles have been won, and campaigns conducted to a successful issue, with less personal exposure to physical danger on the part of the commander-in-chief, than was constantly encountered by Smeaton during the greater part of those years in which the lighthouse was in course of erection. "In all works of danger he himself led the way; was the first to spring upon the rock, and the last to leave it; and by his own example he inspired with courage the humble workmen engaged in carrying out his plans, who, like himself, were unaccustomed to the special terrors of the scene."

We have next to speak of Smeaton's intellectual powers. That they were equal to work of the highest character we have already shown. He was abundantly fertile in resources; no difficulties or obstacles ever embarrassed him; his capacious mind seemed stored with an inexhaustible supply of ingenious expedients. He was the first of the great school of English engineers whose triumphs over nature are recorded in every part of the world. No undertaking ever perplexed that prompt, quick, and massive intellect. Hence his fame has gone on increasing.

James Watt, who always spoke of him in language of warm admiration, calls him "father Smeaton." In justice to him, he writes, "we should observe that he lived before Rennie, and before there were one-tenth of the artists there are now." *Suum cuique*; his example and precepts have made us all engineers.

Robert Stephenson, half a century later, declared him to be the engineer of the highest intellectual eminence that had yet appeared in England. He pronounced him to be "the greatest philosopher in our [the engineering] profession this country has yet produced. He was indeed a great man, possessing a truly Baconian mind, for he was an incessant experimenter. The principles of mechanics were never so clearly exhibited as in his writings, more especially with respect to resistance, gravity, the power of water and wind to turn mills, and so on. His mind was as clear as crystal, and his demonstrations will be found mathematically conclusive.

To this day there are no writings so valuable as his in the highest walks of scientific engineering. When young men ask me, as they frequently do, what they should read, I invariably say, "Go to Smeaton's, philosophical papers; read them, master them thoroughly, and nothing will be of greater service to you. Smeaton was indeed a very great man."

We have said enough to prove that Smeaton was gifted with the most earnest industry, and we have dwelt at some length on his patience, resolution, and perseverance. He was a hard worker throughout his life, from six years old to sixty. And like all hard workers, like all men who have won renown or accomplished great things, he knew how to economize his time; how to utilize every moment; how to employ it in such a manner as to obtain from its use the most advantageous results.

When at home, his forenoons were occupied in writing reports, and in the various transactions connected with his professional engagements; while his afternoons were devoted to the mechanical and scientific pursuits which formed his principal relaxation, working at his forge or in his workshop, making mechanical experiments, or preparing papers on scientific subjects for the Royal Society.

He was endowed by nature with a strong constitution and a robust frame, but there is reason to believe that he tasked his mental powers too laboriously by his intense and continuous application to study during his long periods of seclusion at Austhorpe. As he advanced in years his sturdy strength of limb departed, and his physical powers gave way, while he was yet in his mature manhood. They were further impaired by the abstemious regimen which he was subsequently compelled to adopt. Cerebral disease, moreover, was hereditary in his family, and he long dreaded the attack of paralysis, which eventually terminated his life. But, as Mr. Smiles says, this only made him the more eager to employ to the greatest advantage the time which it might yet be permitted him to live. He dreaded above all things the blight of his mental powers—to use his own words, "lingering over the dregs after the spirit had evaporated"—chiefly as depriving him of the means of doing further good.

The last public measure on which he was professionally

engaged in London was the passing of a Bill through Parliament for the construction of the Birmingham and Worcester Canal. The opposition to it was fierce and protracted, and his support of the measure in committee entailed upon him great application, anxiety, and thought. His friends saw with much concern that the labor was too great for him, and were in constant alarm lest the powers of his vigorous mind should suddenly give way. The Bill, however, passed by a small majority, and Smeaton retired to his house at Austhorpe to enjoy the rest he so greatly needed.

On the 16th of September the blow fell. He was seized with an attack of paralysis while walking in the garden. Happily he regained the use of his mental faculties, and was able to thank the Almighty that his intellect was spared.

During his illness he dictated several letters to his old friend, Mr. Holmes, in which he minutely described his health and feelings. In one of them he says pathetically, "I conclude myself nine-tenths dead, and the greatest favor the Almighty can do (as I think), will be to complete the other part; but as it is likely to be a lingering illness, it is only in his power to say when that is likely to happen,"

Smeaton bore his trial, however, with the equanimity of a Christian, and was very cheerful and resigned. Sometimes he would complain that he had lost his old quickness of apprehension; but recovering himself quickly, he would excuse the momentary impatience, and remark, with a smile, "It could not be otherwise; the shadow must lengthen as the sun goes down." He expressed particular pleasure in seeing the customary occupations of his family resumed, and took the same interest as ever in reading, drawing, music, and conversation. Nor were his remarks less apt or instructive or entertaining than when he was in the flush of health.

One evening he was asked to explain some phenomena respecting the moon, which, from the window of his apartment, could be seen shining in full-orbed splendor. He replied to the questions addressed to him very fully and clearly.

Then, fixing his gaze on the beautiful sphere, he contemplated it steadfastly for some time, observing, "How often have I looked up to it with inquiry and wonder; and how often have I looked forward to the period when I shall have the vast and privileged views of an hereafter, and all will be comprehension and pleasure!"

Smeaton was thus consoled in his last days by the only consolation which, under such circumstances, ever proves effectual, that which flows from a reverent trust in the constant presence of a Divine Father. Though not ostentatious in his religious professions, he had learned the value of religious truth, and he knew that in passing through the valley of the shadow his sole help and support was the mercy of a Redeemer. And hence he listened with delight to the promises of Holy Writ, and joined with fervor in the ministrations of religion.

The great engineer's illness was not of long duration. He passed away on the 28th of October 1792, in the sixty-eighth year of his age.

He was interred with his forefathers in the old parish church of Whitkirk, where a tablet was erected to his memory, bearing the following quaint inscription:

Sacred to the Memory

of

JOHN SMEATON, F.R.S.

A man whom God had endowed with the most extraordinary abilities, which he indefatigably exerted for the benefit of mankind in works of science and philosophical research.

More especially as an Engineer and Mechanic. His principal work, the Eddystone Lighthouse, erected on a rock in the open sea (where one had been washed away by the violence of a storm, and another had been consumed by the rage of fire), secure in its own stability, and the wise precautions for its safety, seems not unlikely to convey to distant ages, as it does to every nation of the Globe, the name of its constructer.

He was born at Austhorpe, June 8, 1724;
And departed this life, October 28, 1792.

Also sacred to the memory of
ANN,
The wife of the said John Smeaton, F.R.S.,
Who died January 17,1784.
Their Two Surviving Daughters,
Duly impressed with sentiments of Love and Respect
for the kindest and tenderest of Parents,
Pay this Tribute to their Memory.

Genius, or originality, is, for the most part, says Hazlitt, some strong quality in the mind, answering to and bringing out some new and striking quality in nature.

According to this definition. Smeaton must be considered a man of genius. But Hazlitt goes on to say that capacity is not the same thing as genius. And he describes capacity as relating to the quantity of knowledge, however acquired; while genius relates to its quality, and the mode of acquiring it. Capacity is the power over given ideas or combinations of ideas; genius is the power over those which are not given, and for which no obvious or precise rule can be laid down,

Smeaton, then, we should prefer to call a man of capacity; a man with a great power over given ideas or combinations of ideas. And along with this capacity he possessed a re-markable steadfastness of purpose, a determined will, an un-conquerable perseverance. Without these adjuncts, indeed, capacity will avail but little. The only motto which it can take up and act upon is that expressed so pithily by the old poet:

See first that the design is wise and just;
That ascertained, pursue it resolutely.
Do not for one repulse forego the purpose
That you resolved to effect.

Smeaton, in his childhood, making turning-lathes and

designing pumps; Ferguson, the boy-astronomer, learning the positions of the stars with the help of a string of beads; Murray, afterwards the eminent Orientalist, teaching himself to write with a blackened brand on the whitewashed wall—these are examples the youthful student should ever set before him. They are examples of what can be done by capacity, directing and controlling diligence, zeal, and application.

A distinguished Italian author has put forward the theory that all men may become great men, may become poets, painters, and orators; as if the sole difference between genius and mediocrity were the power of application. We think it impossible for any calm and sober judgment to accept such a hypothesis. We do not believe that any amount of diligence or perseverance, however continuous and well-directed, could convert a versifier into a Milton, or a blacksmith into a Smeaton.

But then we may all take to ourselves the consolation that it is neither desirable nor necessary that we should all be Smeatons and Miltons. What we have mainly to consider is this—the doing our best in whatever position the will of Providence may have assigned to us, since, by so doing, we may reasonably hope to swell the sum of human happiness and human good.

The benefit we may derive from a study of the career and character of Smeaton is to be found in the encouragement it gives us to lead a life of patient and assiduous labor. For the reader, as for Smeaton, God has provided a vocation, if he will but earnestly seek to discover it; and when he once sees the path of duty before him, he will assuredly gain his reward if he perseveres in it with singleness of aim and loftiness of purpose

If it is not necessary for every man to become a Watt or a Smeaton, and if it is not given to every man to win the success which a Watt or a Smeaton achieved, yet it is possible for each one of us to attain to a certain standard of character and capacity, and to acquire a reasonable measure of prosperity.

As we have elsewhere written, biography is full of examples of what may be accomplished by a resolute will; what may be done by the industry that never wearies, and the energy that never flags. Long and brilliant is the record of men who have attained greatness under the most unfavorable conditions.

The great voyager who opened up a New World to the enterprise of the West was in early life a weaver. The able German historian of the Roman Republic began as a peasant. Sextus V, one of the most capable of the many capable men who have sat in the chair of St. Peter, commenced his career as a swine-herd. Every school-boy knows that Aesop, the most successful of all fabulists, was a slave; Homer,

> The blind old man of Scio's rocky isle

a beggar; and Demosthenes, the orator, whose eloquence controlled the fierce democracy of Athens, the son of a sword-maker. What was Daniel Defoe, the author of the enchanting story of the Solitary in the far-off desert isle, but a hosier's apprentice? Or Gay, the poet and wit, but the drudge of a silk-mercer? James Watt sold spectacles, and invented the present steam-engine; George Stephenson, who began life as a miner's-boy at two shillings per week, founded the railway system of Great Britain; "Rare Ben Jonson," as his epitaph aptly designates him, second among our British dramatists to none but Shakspeare, handled the bricklayer's trowel; and Prideaux, the divine and scholar and critic, was employed to sweep the halls and galleries of Exeter College. Telford, the architect of the Menai Bridge, was a stone-mason's laborer; Rennie, the designer of London Bridge and the Bell-Rock Lighthouse, was the son of a small farmer; Burns, the poet, who walked

> In glory and in joy,
> Behind his plough upon the mountainside.

was a poor cotter's son; Sir Richard Arkwright, the inventor of the power-loom, started in life as a barber; Gifford, the reviewer and critic, as a cobbler.

We see, then, that neither poverty, nor obscure birth, nor unfavorable circumstances in early life, nor lack of friends, nor all the obstacles and difficulties which seem so formidable in the eyes of an ease-loving world, can hold out against the steadfast purpose, against the presence of a clear brain and a courageous heart, determined to work and live and succeed. This is the lesson the preceding pages are intended to enforce; this is the encouragement the story of Smeaton's life should convey to the reader; this is the moral of all Biography, and one which the young should never forget, a moral full

Of courage, hope, and faith!

The Lighthouse

The rocky ledge runs far into the sea,
    And on its outer point, some miles away,
The lighthouse lifts its massive masonry,
    A pillar of fire by night, of cloud by day.

Even at this distance I can see the tides,
    Upheaving, break unheard along its base;
A speechless wrath, that rises and subsides
    In the white lip and tremor of the face.

And as the evening darkens, lo! how bright,
    Through the deep purple of the twilight air,
Beams forth the sudden radiance of its light,
    With strange, unearthly splendor in its glare.

Not one alone; from each projecting cape
    And perilous reef along the ocean's verge,
Starts into life a dim, gigantic shape,
    Holding its lantern o'er the restless surge.

Like the great giant Christopher, it stands
    Upon the brink of the tempestuous wave,
Wading far out among the rocks and sands,
    The night-o'ertaken mariner to save.

And the great ships sail outward and return,
    Bending and bowing o'er the billowy swells;
And ever joyful, as they see it burn,
    They wave their silent welcomes and farewells.

They come forth from the darkness, and their sails
    Gleam for a moment only on the blaze;
And eager faces, as the light unveils,
    Gaze at the tower, and vanish while they gaze.

The mariner remembers when a child,
    On his first voyage, he saw it fade and sink;
Aud, when returning from adventures wild,
    He saw it rise again o'er ocean's brink.

Steadfast, serene, immovable, the same
 Year after year, through all the silent night,
Burns on for evermore that quenchless flame,
 Shines on that unextinguishable light!

It sees the ocean to its bosom clasp
 The rocks and sea-sand with the kiss of peace—
It sees the wild winds lift it in their grasp,
 And hold it up, and shake it like a fleece.

The startled waves leap over it; the storm
 Smites it with all the scourges of the rain;
And steadily against its solid form
 Press the great shoulders of the hurricane.

The sea-bird wheeling round it, with the din
 Of wings and winds and solitary cries,
Blinded and maddened by the light within,
 Dashes himself against the glare, and dies.

A new Prometheus, chained upon the rock,
 Still grasping in his hand the fire of Jove,
It does not hear the cry, nor heed the shock,
 But hails the mariner with words of love.

"Sail on!" it says, "sail on, ye stately ships!
 And with your floating bridge the ocean span;
Be mine to guard this light from all eclipse,
 Be yours to bring man nearer unto man."

LONGFELLOW

For the Finest in
Nautical and Historical
Fiction and Nonfiction

www.FireshipPress.com

Interesting • Informative • Authoritative

Printed in the United States
141961LV00005B/104/P

9 781934 757284